D1122977

Jeffrey pine and western juniper growing out of solid granite
at Olmsted Point, Yosemite National Park.

Willow ptarmigan (*Lagopus lagopus*),
Mount McKinley National Park, Alaska.

Mount Huntington in the Alaska Range is considered by many to be North America's most beautiful mountain. It was not climbed until 1964.

Mule deer (*Odocoilus hemionus*) at Mammoth Hot Springs, Yellowstone National Park.

Yosemite Valley after an early fall snowstorm.

*Next Page:* Moon, mountain, and shadow
rise over the Cirque of the Unclimbables
in Canada's Northwest Territories.

# High and Wild
## A Mountaineer's World

*Photographs and text by*

GALEN ROWELL

Sierra Club Books / San Francisco

BOOKS BY GALEN ROWELL

*The Vertical World of Yosemite*
*In the Throne Room of the Mountain Gods*

Copyright © 1979 by Galen A. Rowell.
All rights reserved. No part of this book may be reproduced in any form or by
any electronic or mechanical means, including information storage and retrieval,
without permission in writing from the publisher.

Portions of this book have appeared in altered form in the *Sierra Club Bulletin,
Quest, Ascent, Backpacker, Mariah,* and the *American Alpine Journal.*

*Library of Congress Cataloging in Publication Data*

Rowell, Galen A.
 High and Wild.

 1. Mountaineering–United States. 2. Mountaineering–Canada. 3. Mountains–
United States–Recreational use. 4. Mountains–Canada–Recreational use.
I. Title
GV191.4.R68     796.5'22'097     79-13000
ISBN: 0-87156-263-4

*The Sierra Club,* founded in 1892 by John Muir, has devoted itself to the study
and protection of the earth's scenic and ecological resources–mountains,
wetlands, woodlands, wild shores and rivers, deserts and plains. The pub-
lishing program of the Sierra Club offers books to the public as a nonprofit
educational service in the hope that they may enlarge the public's understanding of the Club's basic concerns. The point of view expressed in each
book, however, does not necessarily represent that of the Club. The Sierra Club
has some 50 chapters coast to coast, in Canada, Hawaii, and Alaska. For information about how you may participate in its programs to preserve wilderness
and the quality of life, please address inquiries to Sierra Club, *530 Bush Street,
San Francisco, California 94108.*

Printed in the United States of America

FOR NICOLE AND TONY

# CONTENTS

# PREFACE

THIS IS NOT a guidebook. There are plenty of those to tell you what to bring, where to go, and how to get there. The high and wild places of this book are a different kind of wilderness. Wilderness is more than a physical place; it is a state of mind. In fact, it is the original state of mind—the one in which we evolved.

My intent was not only to record images and descriptions of little-known places or adventures. I wanted to provide a different perspective, a more immediate and intuitive view of the activities that form the basis of wilderness exploration: mountain climbing, backpacking, skiing. And thinking.

We have come to think of climbing and skiing as highly competitive. But these activities are far more basic than that: they began as simple methods to reach places otherwise inaccessible. The skills themselves are only tools; they connect us to the world of wilderness. The most sophisticated equipment is only an aid to, not a substitute for, our physical and mental resources. The ability to adapt to things as they are—a practical necessity in wilderness exploration—also teaches us how to live more perceptively. In high and wild places, adventure is life itself.

Galen Rowell

*Berkeley, California*

# Introduction

"I became less and less concerned with the
mastery of technical difficulty,
or even the ascent of individual peaks,
but more and more absorbed in the
problems and delights of movement
over wide areas of mountain country."

ERIC SHIPTON
*That Untravelled World*

Storm approaching the Ruth Glacier, Alaska.

# The New Age of Mountain Exploration

NINE MEN gazed at an endless panorama of snowy mountains glowing softly in the evening sun. Giant glaciers dropped from the flanks of the peaks, covering hundreds of square miles with ice. Except for the men and their equipment, the entire tableau could have been transported from the ice ages of the Pleistocene. The scene's splendor was much more than mere prettiness; it reflected the free expression of natural forces—forces at odds with the men standing for the first time on the summit of Canada's highest mountain, Mount Logan.

A storm was brewing. Black sky oozed toward the men, and they dared not linger at the top, an elevation of nearly 20,000 feet. Mount Logan is more like a range than a single mountain; an eleven-mile section lies above 16,000 feet. The storm overtook the party as it descended in the subarctic twilight, forcing a bivouac in the open at 19,000 feet. The next day they reached their high camp, only to find it torn apart by the blizzard. Another night was spent in the open. When the frostbitten men finally reached their base camp, they found it, too, ravaged by the storm.

At this point, a modern expedition would have radioed a bush pilot, flown out to civilization, and received hospital treatment for frostbite. Even without a radio, the expedition would have faced nothing worse than a boring, painful wait for an aircraft to arrive at a prearranged time.

For the nine men of Albert MacCarthy's successful expedition, however, the ordeal was far from over. The year was 1925, and they were 150 miles from civilization: only a handful of humans had ever seen Mount Logan from closer than fifty miles. In summer the approach to the mountain had been far too rough for pack animals, so MacCarthy and his companions waited until winter snows had carpeted the rugged canyon floors and glacial moraines, and then spent seventy winter days laying in caches over 130 miles of the route. In temperatures that often dipped to −40° F, he and three others slowly worked their way toward the mountain, first using horses, then dog teams when the going got rougher.

Only Greenland and Antarctica are more heavily iced than the thousands of square miles of glaciated highlands surrounding Mount Logan, and both the approach and retreat were like a polar expedition. After forty-four days of ice and snow, MacCarthy's weary party finally touched earth again in June, but the ordeal continued. The expedition decided to speed its retreat by floating the rapids of the Chitina River. Makeshift rafts were built with frostbitten hands, but soon one overturned with men, food, equipment, and cameras aboard. The men swam to safety and completed the long journey to McCarthy, Alaska, on foot.

For the last decade, a high-altitude scientific research camp, supplied by helicopter, has operated each summer at 17,600 feet on Mount Logan. The advent of air travel and modern communication systems have made remoteness increasingly difficult to attain. Remoteness, after all, is more than mere physical distance; it is also a function of psychological and technological separation from the rest of humanity. In time, in

Exploratory mountaineering in Alaska.

isolation, in everything but measured distance, the Logan climbers were more remote than astronauts on the moon.

We are now witnessing the slow death of exploration on earth, and with it the ethos that powered the early polar expeditions and the Mount Logan pioneers. Exploration on foot has become a nostalgic anachronism. Most scientific endeavors associated with it—mapping, surveying, prospecting, photographing, biological research—have welcomed mechanization with open arms. Contemporary climbers use modern transportation and communication to reach the mountains, but they generally agree that the climbing itself must be kept free from motorized or highly technological equipment.

The experience of the first Mount Logan climbers can never be duplicated. Too much of the mountain and its surroundings are too familiar to too many people. But regardless of civilization's encroachment on even the wildest mountain areas, mountaineering has remained essentially a wilderness activity, and its natural setting is all-important. If this were not the case, climbing would be merely an athletic event, as satisfying on tall buildings or inside gymnasiums as on mountains.

It is no accident that many key people in the environmental movement have strong backgrounds in mountaineering, where the very essence of the experience depends on the natural character of the terrain. John Muir, David Brower, Dick Leonard, and Ansel Adams are just a few of the prominent conservationists who climbed mountains extensively, making tangible contacts with the current of evolution and deriving self-knowledge from personal interaction with the harsh, tilted world of rock, snow, ice, and sky. The birth and early years of the Sierra Club took place in this mountain crucible.

Clouds blow across the face of Yosemite's El Capitan, the most continuously vertical cliff in North America.

For many years, I assumed there must be a direct connection between western culture and climbing. Conditioned by American public education, I contented myself with suppositions as arrogant as any entertained by pre-Victorian biologists. I placed great importance on the notion that mountaineering achievements paralleled the growth of industrialized and urban societies. I assumed that climbing was a triumph of rationality over primitive superstition and was the epitome of a goal-oriented society in which events and discoveries had a cumulative value. After all, I had been taught that mankind mastered the world by passing information from generation to generation, enabling modern western man, the latest beneficiary of this process, to understand the basic principles of nature. Armed with such notions, I concluded that only men in this highly evolved and obviously superior state would knowingly expose their mortal bodies to the terrifying forces of nature. I saw climbing as an expression of modern man's understanding of these forces.

I noted that dogs and cats who follow their masters in the mountains seem to have an instinctive sense of where to stop. They might climb one small cliff, but balk completely at one only slightly higher. I attributed this innate prudence to all living things and reasoned that natural selection might favor it. (If this were true, the best climbers would be those with perfectly ordered, logical minds. The opposite is closer to the truth.)

Several events made me re-examine my assumptions about climbers—both animal and human. One occurred in Alaska as a bush pilot flew me to a remote mountain. We flew past the last spruce trees, beyond the final green splotches of alpine vegetation into an arctic world. Wolverine tracks began in the snow and continued for miles to the head of a large glacier, far beyond any source of food. Like our own advance into a hostile environment the tracks seemed unexplainable. I thought I had witnessed an isolated event, but later, I talked to a climber who had seen a single wolf at 10,000 feet on Mount McKinley. Searching for a motive but finding none, I supposed the wolf and the wolverine had merely been lost.

Then I spent a day watching a mountain goat in a wild range of mountains in the Canadian North, and for once I felt I had a clear understanding of nature's logic. Goats climb to avoid predators and to feed on the lush alpine vegetation. I was not at all surprised when my actions in a meadow frightened a goat onto a steep cliff. I watched him run across a headwall on which my companions and I had used ropes and pitons only a few days earlier. With almost sadistic pleasure I approached the bottom of the cliff and guarded the only possible descent from the bulging, 2000-foot rock face. The goat tried every conceivable way of climbing down, but instead of stopping at a point where he began to feel uneasy, he pushed himself, as a climber would, trying something one grade above his standard. I nervously watched him pivot on a hopelessly narrow stance and attempt a traverse that eventually ended in flawless granite. While wandering around the base, I made a discovery: the broken, mummified body of another goat that evidently had fallen from the same cliff. After several hours of watching, I returned to camp, still in sight of the goat, but half a mile away.

Instead of immediately descending and continuing in the direction he was originally headed, the goat stayed on the wall for quite some time. When he did come down, he looked to see if we were still watching. We were too far away to offer any threat to his passage, but he followed the base of the cliff in the direction opposite to

Young Dall ram (*Ovis dalli*) on the north side of Mount McKinley.

where he was originally headed. At the first crack system he began to climb again, this time a flashy, 300-foot romp. At the top of a pedestal he pivoted a full circle, like a fashion model, then bounded down the cliff again. He repeated his climbing antics in other spots, seeming always to make sure that we were watching. Finally, he ambled off in the direction he had originally taken. Where was the instinctive animal prudence I had posited?

The goat's antics appeared to have no survival value. If anything, I thought they merely seemed to be the dangerous frolics of an alpine show-off, but on further reflection I realized my response to the goat's climbing was similar to the public's reaction to human mountaineering. Products of the technological age, we are always ready to condemn as frivolous any activity whose purpose cannot be explained with reason and logic. I knew why I climbed, even if I couldn't express it in words. But as a prisoner of the modern, I believed that the urge had to be logically explainable. "Because it is there!" is a useless platitude. An answer closer to the truth came from a glider pilot who was asked by a television interviewer why he liked to do loops fifty feet above the ground; he simply answered, "I guess I'm just an adrenalin freak!"

Mountaineering may be the final step in terrestrial exploration, but it is increasingly becoming an end in itself. It is futile to explain climbing as either the triumph of rationality over superstition or the triumph of primitiveness over an increasingly artificial world. It is at once neither and both. It is MacCarthy's party on Mount Logan in 1925; crag climbers in New York in 1979; de Saussure making scientific observations on Mont Blanc in 1787; sourdoughs climbing Mount McKinley's north peak in 1910; Whymper, who longed to be a polar explorer, climbing the Matterhorn in 1865; Whillans, a Manchester plumber, on Mount Everest in 1972; two children scrambling in a national park campground; Toni Egger disappearing on Cerro Torre in icy Patagonia; an Indian hunting party on top of Mount Whitney; a solo climber on Yosemite's El Capitan.

The common thread of these diverse experiences is human interaction with mountains. But not all such interaction is considered mountaineering. The north wall of the Eiger is one of the most famous climbs in Europe, but those who traverse it via the railway tunnel that pierces its face can hardly be called mountaineers. Climbers adapt their behavior to wild surroundings rather than changing the face of the land to ease their passage. Most questions of climbing ethics and style revolve around this concept. Techniques that alter the environment—even temporarily—are not considered as good style as those that leave no sign of passage. Examples of environment-altering techniques are step-cutting in ice; expansion bolts, which require holes drilled into rock; expeditionary climbing, which depends on establishing temporary tent cities at strategic locations and moving a pyramid of men and supplies upward until the summit is within easy striking distance; and the use of fixed ropes, which enable climbers to ascend the rope instead of the rock or snow.

Unlike skiing, kayaking, and many other outdoor sports, climbing is not fundamentally dependent on equipment. A skier can't ski without skis, but a climber can climb without ropes or pitons. Much climbing is done without any special equipment at all. At least half of the five hundred "technical" climbs in Yosemite Valley could be climbed solo, unroped and barefoot, by a highly skilled climber, although this would be as risky as a circus acrobat performing without a net. The next step beyond climbing without equipment is to carry it only for safety—as an acrobat uses his net for security—rather than for direct climbing aid. This is often the most satisfying kind of climbing: raw adventure achieved with a few classic tools. Simplicity is the hallmark of good climbing equipment. A nylon climbing rope is a simple tool that does a complex job. It is a flexible, portable, energy-absorbing device capable of diffusing sudden shock loads of thousands of pounds. Similarly, an ice axe serves as a step-cutting tool, a walking stick, a handhold for technical ice-climbing, and a braking mechanism for a climber falling on snow. By shifting the emphasis from working with the natural scene to tinkering with gear, equipment fetishists alter the basic character of the mountaineering experience.

Collecting an excess of fancy new equipment, however pointless in itself, is only one symptom of a more serious ailment. Perhaps because they can no longer look forward to the rewards of explorers, modern climbers feel compelled to measure themselves in other ways—usually not so much by skill and dedication as by lists of conquests. Climbs are numbered, measured, and categorized; and for many, the goal becomes all-important, the game only secondary. What Aleister Crowley, the eccentric Englishman, stated early in the century holds true today: "Climbing itself is being very much spoilt by the attitude of the [British] Alpine Club in insisting that the achievement, not the enjoyment, is the important thing. This is the American Spirit, to count and compare instead of being content with spiritual satisfaction."

Crowley may have overstated his case, for spiritual satisfaction is a synergism involving both self-experience and achievement. And competition is often a necessary catalyst for the biggest climbs, providing motivation for an activity that is useless in practical terms. But he is right that the self-knowledge derived from personal interaction with natural forces is a more important component of alpinism than is competition with the rated and timed achievements of others.

Nearing the summit overhangs on the northwest face of Half Dome, Yosemite Valley.

The renowned British climber, A. F. Mummery, who climbed in the Alps a century ago, once wrote:

> The true Mountaineer is the man who attempts new ascents. Equally, whether he succeeds or fails, he delights in the fun and jollity of the struggle. The gaunt, bare slabs, the square, precipitous steps in the ridge, and the black, bulging ice of the gully, are the very breath of life to his being. I do not pretend to be able to analyze this feeling, still less to be able to make it clear to unbelievers. It must be felt to be understood, but it is potent to happiness and sends the blood tingling through the veins, destroying every trace of cynicism and striking at the very roots of pessimistic philosophy.

Mummery sounds a theme that is becoming increasingly popular today: The true mountaineer, whether he succeeds or fails, delights in the struggle. Of course there is

Ski touring on the Ruth Glacier below the Moose's Tooth, Alaska.

Yosemite's "natural firefall."
This phenomenon occurs only on a few days
in February of each year, when sunset
strikes Horsetail Fall on El Capitan
after the cliff is in shadow.

some extra elation in a hard-won achievement, but the emphasis is more on the effort itself than on its ends. The first ascent of a mountain is only the beginning. Almost endless variations are possible: new routes, solo climbs, winter climbs, all-free ascents, pitonless ascents, alpine-style climbs of mountains previously climbed by expeditionary sieges. Many of the adventures described in this book represent "new twists" to old challenges and are all the more rewarding for being so.

Many young climbers feel unlucky not to have been part of the so-called Golden Age, roughly from 1860 to 1960, when most of the world's important mountains and rock walls were climbed for the first time. These particular achievements can never be repeated, but a mountain or cliff is never conquered, though one party of climbers or many manage to sneak through its defenses. Crowley's "spiritual satisfaction" and Mummery's "delight in the struggle" are still available for the modern generation, for the 2000th person on top of Mount McKinley as well as for the first, and for the unnumbered person who solves a boulder problem in a city park.

Every present-day mountaineer is a frustrated explorer at heart, secretly envying the struggles of the Mount Logan climbers and other pioneers of the high wilderness. He intuitively comprehends the mysterious attraction of alpine sanctuaries for the wolverine, the wolf, and the mountain goat. Also intuitively, he plays the climbing games of style without ever having been taught the rules. If he were told he must play the games according to a fixed set of rules, he would surely rebel. He values first ascents, but is more often found doing "old classics" for the sheer joy of climbing. His experiences, not medallions, are his achievements. When he does throw his heart and soul into an especially difficult climb, he feels not only joy, but also regret when it is over. Like Mummery, he delights in the struggle, and many lowland hours are spent in contemplation of his next objective.

The remoteness of Mount Logan in 1925 is gone forever, but a glimpse through the window of the past is still possible. A glint is returning to some climbers' eyes as they go after famed Himalayan mountains in self-contained, alpine-style groups. The trend of not using hammers in rockclimbing leaves many newer routes with no signs of human passage; every person who repeats these climbs can discover them anew, as did the first ascent party. The limiting factor in mountaineering is not first ascents but wilderness, and prime experiences will always be dependent on the preservation of the environment.

This book depicts and celebrates only a few of North America's high and wild places—those I have been privileged to visit. The events reported here are only episodes in the developing drama of mountaineering. As long as wild places remain unchanged by the hand of man, adventurers will continue to experience them in ever-changing ways.

# High and Wild

"That new vision of the world won through hardship . . ."

ANTOINE DE SAINT-EXUPÉRY

Clearing storm over El Capitan, Yosemite Valley.

# 1 / *Alone on Bear Creek Spire*

ON a Friday evening in 1971 I drove two hundred miles east from Berkeley, California, on a road as familiar to me as my home street. It led to Yosemite Valley, where I had been climbing on weekends for a decade. As the winding road enters the national park, it parallels the Merced River through a deep gorge, and the canyon broadens into a flat valley surrounded by cliffs that rise to the stars.

Even to those who have been there hundreds of times, the first glimpse of Yosemite is overwhelming. As a child I imagined that the valley at night looked like a movie set. Moonlight reflected from the massive granite forms made them appear too stark and simple to be big; the valley seemed like a small model of itself. I felt I could almost reach out and touch the tops of cliffs three thousand feet overhead.

I stopped at Yosemite Lodge, where I met a group of climbers who gathered there every weekend. Within minutes I was invited to join friends on a route I had done many times before. Though I had intended to climb in Yosemite, I felt a sudden urge to change that plan and suggested an alternative—the south face of Bear Creek Spire in the John Muir Wilderness adjoining Yosemite National Park. No interest. I might as well have suggested Patagonia.

I sat and thought for a while about why I had lost enthusiasm for a Yosemite climb, and soon realized that I felt a need to escape the security Yosemite represented. It was home—familiar walls, faces, sounds, smells—and I was already part of an earlier generation, from a time when climbers knew the wonder of gazing at great cliffs still untouched by the hand of man. When I first climbed in Yosemite in 1957, none of the big walls had been ascended. Since that time, all of Yosemite's major cliffs had been climbed by at least one route; El Capitan now had eleven; the front face of Half Dome, four. The simple joys of exploration were on the wane; in their place was a trend to count and compare experiences with those of others who had climbed the same routes. I had no doubt that many Yosemite climbs demanded greater skill than the hardest routes of the highest ranges, but a big red flag went up when I saw climbers far more talented than myself unwilling to test in the nearby wilderness the skills acquired in this fair-weather womb. There was little I could do personally to reverse what I considered an unfortunate trend, except to bow out of it. I decided to go to Bear Creek Spire, alone. The decision to solo did not come from any high motive; quite simply, no one would go with me.

I slept fitfully in a crowded campground before driving at dawn toward Tioga Pass, on the park's eastern boundary. The pass, at almost 10,000 feet, was just below timberline; and though summer was nearly over, the meadows were still lush. My climb would begin in just this sort of terrain, but farther south, where not a single road crossed the rugged Sierra crest for two hundred miles. To reach my starting point I drove another hundred miles, first dropping thousands of feet to the desert floor of the Mono Basin, then along the base of the mountains until a deadend side road brought me back up to 10,400 feet.

Here I locked my ten-speed bicycle to a tree in the woods not far from the roadhead. My plan was to drive on to another trailhead farther south, walk eight miles in and 5000 feet up to the base of Bear Creek Spire, climb it, traverse the north side to pick up my bicycle, and ride forty miles back to my car.

From where I cached my bike, I could see Bear Creek Spire about ten miles away, and before turning around to continue south, I took a long look at it. I had once wondered why this undistinguished 13,713-foot peak, which had been climbed from the west by a moderate scramble in 1923, was named a spire. The answer was clear when I first saw its south face from the ridge of another mountain. The face is a pointed blade of granite, which to the best of my knowledge had never been attempted.

I drove on into America's deepest valley, the Owens Valley, created by a massive fault block between the 14,000-foot summits of the High Sierra and the White Mountains twenty miles to the east. An earthquake greater than the one that almost destroyed San Francisco in 1906 dropped the valley twenty feet in 1872. I took a side road up Pine Creek to the largest tungsten mine in North America. Outwardly it looks like a normal mining operation in a mountain valley; actually, it is upside-down. Shafts climb from the tunnels up into the mountains, and one penetrates Bear Creek Spire, four air miles away.

I left my car and began hiking away from the creaks and whines of the milling operation. I soon came upon what looked like a natural marble quarry: glacial polish had combined with frost-heaving to segment white aplite into piles of burnished

Aspen and wild rose,
Little Lakes Valley.

Immature great horned owl (*Bubo virginianus*) in a rock crevice on the east slope of the High Sierra.

Aerial view
of the south face
of Bear Creek Spire.

blocks that gleamed against the surrounding granite. By noon I left the last whitebark pines below and set out across a barren moraine composed of loose granite boulders. When I saw the vivid green of a tiny lake set amid the glacial debris, I knew that ice somewhere beneath the surface was still carving this landscape. Glacially scoured rock dust—"glacier milk"—accounted for the water's tint.

My memory of how impressive the south face appeared from a distance had been tempered somewhat by a recent look at the contour map, which showed the wall to be about 800 feet high and not particularly steep. Now, at close range, my original impression returned; the face was fully 1200 feet high, without a single large ledge. The situation gave me pause. It was two o'clock in the afternoon, and I was carrying only minimal equipment: a ⅜-inch rope, one quart of water, some food, a short, half sleeping bag, and a handful of pitons and carabiners. I foresaw a demanding afternoon on the face under a hot sun, but nothing to make me seriously consider giving up the ascent.

The climbing began with deceptive ease. I didn't even rope up for several hundred feet, because cracks and handholds kept appearing in just the right places. A squeeze chimney at nearly 13,000 feet left me panting, however; and I used rope and pitons for safety on the steep face above. I made steady progress until I reached a small pedestal and discovered a smooth headwall above; I tried to free-climb it with the rope for safety, but failed. The only crack I could spot was separated from better terrain above by about eight feet of blank overhanging rock.

Dropping back to the top of the pedestal, I drank the last of my water and thought about Yosemite. My bright idea of a remote climb was losing its luster rapidly. I could picture my friends in the Valley, who had probably come down from their routes before the afternoon heat, and were now sitting in the restaurant with a drink or cavorting in Camp Four, the Yosemite climbers' camp. I, on the other hand, contemplated a cold night at 13,000 feet and an arduous descent in the morning.

After a brief rest, I clipped a sling into my highest piton and stood in it. The overhanging wall pushed me out, and after a futile effort to surmount it, I descended again. The sun was about to leave the face, and I knew that my best chance was to give

Technical rockclimbing
on Yosemite's
"Lunatic Fringe."

it everything I had while the rock was still warm. This time I put the shortest possible loop into the piton so I could stand a bit higher than before. The headwall had a shallow vertical groove; and I worked, with my elbow pointed skyward, to secure an arm-lock between my inverted palm and shoulder. When I tried to move my free leg, I felt completely helpless, but I made one final attempt. Dangling from the overhang by the arm-lock, I pulled my foot away from the security of the loop and up onto the eye of the piton. The extra inches let me move the arm-lock higher. I was now out of balance, but very near a wide crack, and a desperate lunge took me high enough to jam a fist into the bottom of the crack.

Relief surged through me, as though a gun aimed at my head had just misfired. The danger was not entirely over, however; I knew that my adrenalin-stimulated strength would be short-lived. I continued up, fist-jamming thirty feet to a narrow ledge, and panted there for long minutes. The ledge traversed the steep headwall for a hundred feet and then connected with a chimney system. It was a lucky break; I wouldn't need to bivouac on the cliff if I could move efficiently in the minutes remaining before dark.

The day's harsh sunlight gave way to dusk, and in the indirect light I could see into the shadowy north faces of an endless sea of peaks. It was a more rugged Sierra vista than I had ever known in summer. At my feet were alpine flowers; this very contrast of life and barren rock had led John Muir to call the range "the gentle wilderness."

All along the ledge yellow hulsea and purple polemonium were still in bloom. Sierra bighorn sheep depend on them as an important part of their summer diet. In Muir's day, the flowers might have been nibbled down to the roots. Weathered horns and ancient Indian hunting blinds attest to the fact that the bighorn, now a threatened

Alpine meadow
in the High Sierra.

These bighorn sheep are members of a threatened subspecies (*Ovis canadensis californicus*), only a few hundred of which still survive in the High Sierra.

species, once ranged as high as the very tops of most mountains along the crest. I could imagine a ram profiled on the summit ramparts only a hundred feet above me as I hurried along the ledge below.

Having reached the chimney, I climbed steadily with the pack suspended below me, and within minutes I was standing on the summit in the last rays of the sun. I would have liked to linger, but it was late. I scrambled toward the shadows of the north side, heading down the broken face toward a tiny meadow with a stream. An hour later, in the dark, I bent down for my first drink in many hours.

I had planned to stop by the stream for only a minute, then descend in the moonlight to the forest below, but after eating a package of freeze-dried hash mixed with cold water, I realized that my legs didn't want to support my body any longer. Without standing up again, I crawled into my half-bag. Though extremely fatigued, I lay sleepless for hours, still carried along by the forced awareness the day had demanded. I felt lucky to have made the climb and to have gotten down safely. I no longer envied the climbers loafing around the Yosemite campground. I was content where I was, alone under the stars on a clear night.

Sunrise under a mantle of cloud strikes the high desert of the Owens Valley.

I set off again before dawn, walking through Little Lakes Valley toward the roadhead. After a single day high in the mountains, the well-used trail and established campsites seemed like civilization. At sunrise I reached the trailhead where my bicycle was cached and soon reveled in a 6000-foot downhill ride. From the floor of Owens Valley I had to climb again, struggling up a 3000-foot grade in desert heat that was already intense. I stopped half a dozen times to plunge my upper body into mountain streams. At nine that morning, less than twenty-four hours after starting up the trail toward Bear Creek Spire, I reached my car, with barely enough energy left to lift the light ten-speed inside.

A solo climb such as the one I had just made is not a logical extension of Yosemite technique, which stresses extending limits of ability while protected by equipment. Nor is solo climbing simply the means to an end, for there are far easier ways to reach summits. It is a form of private, heightened awareness—something that anyone who has spent time alone under stress can understand. What makes it different and desirable is doing so by choice.

# 2 / *The Great White Throne*

DURING the 1960s climbers who wanted to ascend the legendary sandstone towers of the American desert faced almost as many restrictions as travelers wishing to visit Eastern Europe. Access to the best climbs was forbidden by either government agencies or the Navajo tribe, which, after a century of oppression, had begun to reassert itself. Visitors were required to pay a fee to enter reservation lands, and climbing was outlawed on the sacred cliffs of Monument Valley and Shiprock. The 2000-foot cliffs of Zion Canyon, in southern Utah, were also off-limits because of a ruling by the National Park Service. Although roped ascents of the easiest sides of the formations were permitted, attempts on the great walls had been banned; park rangers judged the soft sandstone unsafe for Yosemite-style sieges, during which climbers must live on a wall for days.

Fred Beckey was the most ubiquitous North American climber of the postwar era. The veteran of a thousand routes—mostly first ascents—Fred had a reputation for succeeding through persistence rather than by unusual skill. Difficulties that held back other climbers—trailless approaches, blank headwalls, miserable weather—seemed only to increase his determination. Fred wanted to climb the 2200-foot northwest face of the Great White Throne, Zion's most famous landmark. He first applied for permission in 1965 and was turned down, but this failed to deter him. Reasoning that bureaucracy thrives on a constant diet of paper, he began a stream of correspondence to the park service director, the regional office, the superintendent, the chief ranger, assorted secretaries, and undoubtedly a garbage collector or two. Each letter was duly and courteously answered, and Fred in turn would respond, *ad infinitum*. Ultimately, he wore down the agency's resistance, and special permission was granted on the conditions that the climbers maintain radio communication with the ground and have a rescue party available.

In early April of 1967 I joined Fred and Pat Callis in Zion. Our support party consisted of Pat's wife and Harry Woodworth, a friend of mine from California. Their job was to operate the ground radio and to call the Tacoma Mountain Rescue Team if necessary.

We were gratified to find firm rock on the cliffs at the bottom of the canyon. The same rock, Navajo Sandstone, is found in varying degrees of hardness throughout the Southwest. During the Permian epoch, the Zion area was covered by an inland sea. When those waters retreated, one of the world's largest deserts began to form. For millions of years, however, the climate was still wet enough to leach iron oxide from the distant mountains. Great sand dunes covered the landscape, and sedimentary rock formed at their bases as calcium carbonate—lime—mixed with iron oxide to weld grains of sand together. Later on, the climate became drier; rain no longer washed iron oxide from the hills, and only pure carbonate glued the particles together.

The Great White Throne stood before us like a cross-sectional illustration in a textbook. Shaped like a brick standing on end, its lower third was fiery red, and the

The Totem Pole in Monument Valley, one of the most spectacular eroded sandstone pinnacles of the Southwest.

upper sections were whiter than Yosemite granite. At its base was the tiny Virgin River, which had cut two thousand feet through rock over eons of time. Smaller side streams had carved the other sides of the Throne, creating a monolith that stood independent of the other canyon walls. All the cliffs were striped in white and red bands, and we understood why the tourist brochures proclaimed Zion "Yosemite Valley in Color."

We didn't expect the quality of the rock to match the area's scenic beauty, but we were pleasantly surprised to begin the climb on firm rock with continuous cracks. On the first lead I protected a long lieback with several pitons driven as solidly as possible. Pat had trouble hammering them out, which increased our confidence in the rock's strength. Higher up I drilled two expansion bolts into crackless rock and found that it took nearly as long as it would have to drill into granite. We came down that evening, leaving fixed ropes up to our high point. The next day we reached a forested ledge in the center of the face late in the day. Since the weather had begun to look bad, we descended again.

A fast-moving cold front passed through that night, covering the mountains with snow, and we awoke to clearing skies in a fairyland of frosted sandcastles. Two days later we started our final push. Several hours of climbing brought us to our old high point, where Fred began leading a vertical crack using direct aid. The character of the rock changed abruptly. Gone was the hard red sandstone, and now we encountered gray rock that crumbled to pieces in our hands. Fred's pitons sank like nails driven into soft bark. When he could no longer make a piton hold his weight, he drilled a hole for an expansion bolt. The quarter-inch drill made a rounded pit big enough for his little finger. "This stuff is like brown sugar," he yelled down. "There's no way we can continue with the equipment we have."

Our afternoon radio call brought a forecast of a series of storms. We descended again and called a council of war. Apparently, the impure lime that held together the white sandstone of the upper cliffs was partly water soluble. The red rock was far more sound to begin with and relatively unaffected by the moisture. Fred had tried the old desert trick of drilled-in angles—driving a three-quarter-inch sawed-off piton into a quarter-inch drilled hole—but the sharp edges of the piton broke the rock away, and none of us felt safe trusting our lives to such devices. We decided to go home for a few weeks and return when the weather had stabilized and the rock was dry. I would make up a batch of new anchors that could be twisted into drilled holes where the rock was soft. Fred would monitor the weather and call us when the time was right.

I had the opportunity to observe one of Fred's weather checks when he visited my automotive shop shortly after we returned to California. Never one to waste money, Fred used a pay phone to make a toll-free call to directory assistance in southern Utah. When the operator came on, he asked her what the weather was like. She replied that she didn't have that information and offered him the weather number. "No, no, I don't need that," Fred told her. "Just look out your window and tell me if there are any clouds. And is it windy? How warm is it? Operator? Operator?"

The operator hung up, but Fred patiently tried again and again, until he persuaded someone to look out the window. He repeated this process daily, and also checked the newspaper weather maps. It proved to be the worst spring in thirty years. The usual high pressure zone over the Great Basin never became established, and a battery of storms from the Pacific marched continuously inland.

The Great White Throne after a spring snowfall,
with every ledge and crevice standing out in relief.

Pat Callis climbing with direct aid on the upper face of the Great White Throne.

Fred sounded the bugle at last in early May, and we met in Zion under clouds. With a prediction for clearing skies we returned to our high point, where Pat took over the lead on Fred's "brown-sugar" pitch. It was overcast and still as Pat climbed Fred's ladder of pitons, but as soon as he ventured onto new ground we witnessed the most sudden change in weather I had ever seen. Pat described his experience:

The sky became dark and from far below came the wailing of a violent wind rushing up the canyon floor, bending the trees and whipping the water of the river. Lightning, thunder, and suddenly the air was full of swirling snow. I stood in my slings as though in a trance, fascinated and frightened by the swiftness in which the storm had transformed our world into a hostile place. The storm seemed to magnify the distance between my belayer and myself, and I felt alone and frail. Meekly, I retreated down the snow-choked crack in a puppet-like response to the beckoning of my companions.

In a matter of a few minutes, the fierce squall moved on; and the sun came out. Pat finished his lead, and I spent several hours working up a straightforward crack with direct aid. Such a stretch could have been climbed in minutes on Yosemite granite. Tap a piton a couple of times; clip in the rope and a sling; stand higher; tap another. Here each piton placement had to be laboriously prepared. Sometimes I would beat on a piton for several minutes, only to have it fall out loosely in my hand. Then I would drive a bigger one into the slot. At best it took about a hundred hard bashes to drive a two-inch blade into a crack, and we were both exhausted by the end of the day. We rappelled 400 feet and joined Fred in a camp with a fire on a spacious ledge.

The following day we hauled loads of food, equipment, and water up to "Last Chance Ledge," six hundred feet from the summit. Above lay the crux of the route. A curving open book stretched from the summit to about two hundred fifty feet above our ledge, but the area in between was overhanging and quite blank. We were gratified, though, to find thin cracks leading up the headwall. Fred and Pat spent the remainder of the day on two painfully slow leads. Fred just reached the open book as alpenglow turned the upper face into the color of a living ember.

We returned to Last Chance Ledge that night, and in the morning I went up to take the first lead. On the overhanging soft rock I had considerable trouble finding decent cracks for pitons. Fred persuaded me to use nylon loops tied around the inch-thick trunk of a decaying juniper that stuck out of a crack, claiming that any tree with greenery on it would hold a man's weight. I put a tie-off loop around the trunk, cautiously pulled on it, attached a sling, and stepped up. At first the tree held my weight—but just as Fred was telling me that the more I climbed, the more I would learn to trust trees that grew on cliffs, there was a loud snap. The tree broke off, and I flew through the air with it attached to the rope just above me. Fred's belay through a lower piton stopped me after a 30-foot fall. Since the face was overhanging, I was unhurt, except where the tree slid down the rope and scratched me. I untied it and watched it fall the full distance to the desert floor below.

I tried the same spot again and took another fall when a soft foothold broke. On the third day I slowly drilled my way past the tree stump using lag screws. Three hundred feet of easier climbing put us on a big ledge near the top. The last lead went up steeply for fifteen feet, and we expected it to gradually round off onto the summit. At the top of the little headwall, our climb ended with stunning abruptness. One second I was over the big drop; the next I was walking on a plateau. By sunset we had all of the party and equipment on top.

We had never visited such a mountain summit. Inaccessible except by technical climbing, it was a level island of desert, half a mile wide. It had been reached only a few times by seven hundred feet of rockclimbing from the south side. Park rangers had told us a little about the natural history of this lofty mesa. A lightning fire here a few years back had been allowed to burn itself out, leaving the top more barren than the surrounding high desert plateau. Somehow, several species of mammals frequented this island of desert. One party had sighted a bobcat on top. We saw chipmunks during the day and a kangaroo rat at night. The scuffling sound of a larger animal near our fire led us to the tracks of a ringtail cat.

The top of the Throne was quite a liveable place except for the absence of water. Only small rodents, specially adapted to extracting liquid from their food, could live

The secretive mountain lions (*Felis concolor*) of the American West offer no threat to wilderness travelers. This youngster is less than a year old.

here year-round. We wondered how these animals, residents and visitors alike, had come here. One biologist has theorized that predatory birds carried up any rodents that now live on top. Although none of us had degrees in natural history, our experience led us to distrust complex solutions that ignored the obvious. We suspected that, rather than being airlifted, these animals had simply done as we had: climbed under their own power. Climbers in every part of the world have come back with unusual animal sightings. The *yeti* tracks found by Eric Shipton in the Himalayan snows have yet to be satisfactorily explained, but there is little doubt, for example, that a large climbing party on Mount Rainier really did watch a black bear casually step onto the summit, turn around, and head back down the miles of crevassed glaciers. We all had seen rats high on Yosemite cliffs, even in the middle of El Capitan where crack systems didn't appear to connect.

In the morning we set up seven 150-foot rappels to descend the back side. Reaching the main valley would have taken twenty more rappels, so we traversed across the high country toward a highway four miles away. Following heavily used deer trails over exposed sandstone, we could easily imagine a desperado behind every rock. At one spot that would have been perfect for a B-movie ambush, I came across a freshly killed deer and cat tracks as big as my fist angling toward a ravine. A mountain lion had made the kill and was probably watching us from a safe distance, waiting to return when we left.

The transition to civilization was as abrupt as reaching the summit had been. Around a corner, sage and trailless sandstone ran smack into a highway. That evening we were treated to a victory dinner by the only restaurant in the nearest town, and on the way out I passed Fred Beckey using the pay phone. "Anchorage information? What's the weather like up there? No, just look out your window . . ."

# 3 / *The South Face of Half Dome*

HALF DOME is not really half a dome. From every point in Yosemite Valley, with no strain on the imagination, one sees the perfect image of its name, but viewed from the rear its true form becomes apparent. Instead of the rounded south wall one expects, there is a steep cliff, slightly higher and far more flawless than the famous front, or northwest, face. Half Dome actually is a whole dome with a character unlike any other dome in America.

Half Dome, seen here during the clearing of a winter storm, rises nearly 5000 feet above Yosemite Valley.

Until 1870 geologists argued convincingly that Yosemite's cliffs had been formed by the bottom dropping out of the valley, and that Half Dome must have been whole until one side was sheared off in some primeval cataclysm. After John Muir studied Yosemite, however, he wrote that the "Master Builder" had chosen "not the earthquake nor lightning to rend and split asunder . . . but tender snowflowers falling noiselessly eon after eon, the offspring of the sun and the sea." Muir's glacial theory proved closer to the truth than the cataclysmic one, but modern geologists have discovered that the greater part of Half Dome was never glaciated. Ice gave the dome its clean appearance by scouring debris from the base, but its basic form is the result of gradual processes that were well under way before the ice ages.

Half Dome can be likened more accurately to the last joint of a thumb than to the cleaved hemisphere the name suggests. The textures of its sides are as different as a thumbnail and a fingerprint. The northwest face is laced with crack systems produced by vertical joints—lines of structural weakness—cast into the granite as it cooled. The incredibly smooth surface of the south face is due to the total absence of such joints. The northwest is shady and streaked with lichens; the south bakes all day in the sun.

The south face of Half Dome
is the smoothest big cliff
in North America.

A climber crawls across "Thank-God Ledge," near the top of Half Dome's northwest face. The cleanly fractured rock here contrasts sharply with the south side.

I was introduced to the true character of the south face by Warren Harding, who had made first ascents of many of the biggest Yosemite faces. By 1965 the back side of Half Dome, unseen except from trails above the Valley, was the last major unclimbed cliff in the park. Warren invited me to join him on a winter reconnaissance that he hoped would lead, later that year, to a full-scale attempt on the face. We planned to scout a climbing route by observing where fresh snow demarked cracks and ledges on the face, but after a four-mile walk to the base of the south face, we found ourselves staring at a vertical desert. No snow clung to the wall. It was devoid of features except for a single overhanging arch that ended in blankness.

Though Warren and I suspected that the south face might be the smoothest big cliff in the world, we never imagined that the ascent would ultimately require six attempts spread over five years—more actual climbing time than any of the dozen Himalayan or Alaskan climbs I've taken part in since. It was also an ascent that violated many of mountaineering's unwritten rules about style and technique. Climbs considered classics are rarely the most difficult routes but rather are ones that follow unexpected geologic weaknesses through seemingly impregnable terrain. The climber's joy in a classic first ascent has much in common with that of the research scientist who has made a ground-breaking discovery: it rests chiefly in the "elegance" of finding a simple solution to a complex problem. To preserve this experience, climbers have generally agreed that drilling ladders of bolts is justified only to connect natural weaknesses, not as a major element of an ascent.

Warren never believed in following a prescribed ethic; he thought each person should choose his or her own brand of mountain madness. He had used one hundred bolts on otherwise unclimbable sections of the first route up El Capitan in 1958, and he estimated that 150 or so might be needed on the south face of Half Dome. We both considered this technique justified in making the first route up an especially blank wall.

On the first attempt in June 1966, we were joined by Yvon Chouinard and Chuck Pratt. After a close look at the face's terrible smoothness, Chouinard wanted to withdraw—not because of the difficulty but because of his dislike for the amount of artificial aid that would be needed. He stayed for the first pitch, during which he took a short fall, complained of an injured shoulder, and quit. A week later, with Gary Colliver along, we made another attempt. Gary rappelled down after one bivouac, but Warren and I continued on for three more days, following a crack system on the underside of the great arch. We felt as though we were ascending the inside of a 900-foot peaked roof. Our reward for surmounting this obstacle was a two-day wait in a storm, hanging inside an eighteen-inch slot. At the end of this ordeal Warren was still eager to go on, but it was now my turn to plead the cause of retreat on the grounds of a bad cold. We made no further attempts on the south face that year.

Warren's work kept him out of the country for the next year. When he returned, he began designing his now-legendary "Bat" equipment—the acronym stands for Basically Absurd Technology—for another go at the south face. Our living quarters would be Bat tents: single-point suspension, one-person, fully enclosed, semi-waterproof hammocks. Our progress over blank rock would be speeded by the use of Bathooks, tiny steel hooks that could be wedged into holes only one-third the depth required for bolts. Even the name Warren Harding was no longer distinctive enough for the inventor of the Bat gadgets; Warren rechristened himself "Batso."

Aerial view of the south face in winter. The overhanging arch in the center is the
only prominent feature on this unbroken and nearly vertical side of the dome.

As we studied photo blow-ups of the face, the ascent began to take on an aura of fantasy. The dome itself resembled a giant bald head; its most obvious features were three closely spaced black spots that we named the Tri-clops Eye. Above this strange triple eye was a zone of darker rock that became known as the Gray Matter. Warren fantasized that the Tri-clops Eye was the entrance to a huge amphitheater in the center of the dome. When we reached it, we would be able to peer inside and see all the gods of the ancients seated around a table. Janus, the two-headed god of doorways, would be on hand to say, "Come in—we've been expecting you!"

In November 1968, after five days of climbing and fifty Bathooks drilled into flawless rock, Warren and I reached the right-hand eye of the Tri-clops. Our imaginary amphitheater vanished in the face of reality: we found neither cave nor ledge—in fact, barely a dent in the armorplate. The reality proved exciting enough, however. As we set up our Bat tents for yet another night on the face, nature was changing the sets in preparation for a wild scene. Cirrus clouds raced by overhead, billowing cumulus hung over the High Sierra to the east, and a seething mass of cloud oozed up from the floor of the canyon below, moving sporadically like a giant amoeba. Darkness and the white mass overcame us simultaneously. At midnight we were awakened by raindrops, at four it began snowing, and by dawn everything was white.

Peering outside our Bat tents, we saw that our vertical wall was plastered with a thick layer of wet snow. As the day warmed, we witnessed a striking demonstration of how the Tri-clops were formed. They were focal points for drainage on the upper wall. Soon both of us were in the middle of a temporary waterfall and soaked to the skin. The hours came and went with painful slowness. Our Bat tents were indeed watertight: water seeped in where they touched the rock, but it didn't seep out. Our sleeping bags became thin bags of nylon with lumps of wet goose down coagulated near the bottom. We punctured holes in the floor of the tents for drainage, shivered continuously, and prayed for sun. At noon we conferred via small walkie-talkies with our support party on the trail to the south of us, and were advised that no major storm was forecast. Assuming our weather to be a local disturbance, we decided to wait it out, while our friends walked down to the Valley in the rain.

Warren Harding
high on the south face.

Warren Harding
near the final bivouac
on the south face.

Small avalanches struck us as we hung motionless. Fingers and toes numbed, and our skin became as wrinkled as a prune. After another night and morning passed, the air grew colder and still the storm continued. Warren wanted to stay, but I wanted to descend; I didn't want to die without a fight, and the choices seemed absurdly clear: November snow, hypothermia, and frostbite versus a warm fire and a filet mignon dinner. Finally I yelled over the howling wind, "Warren, we have to go down!"

"We?" came the answer. "I've played that game before, and I'm not moving anywhere."

I pouted for a while, and, considering the odds of freezing if I stayed, decided to descend alone. I figured that it would take about ten rappels with a doubled rope which I would have to pull down by one end after each descent in order to set up the following rappel. I said goodbye to Warren and promised him help as soon as I reached the Valley. Disappearing down the wall, I realized that I would need to swing across the face for a few feet in order to reach the next anchor point. Eight feet below the Tri-clops, however, I discovered that I couldn't move out of the plumb line of the rope. The rock was coated with ice, and further testing showed that the rappel rope was frozen in place at the top and wouldn't pull down.

I was in a far more serious position than the one I had just left above in the Tri-clops eye. Constant powder avalanches knocked me about and filled my supposedly waterproof clothing as if by osmosis. I became infinitely cold, and my thoughts went from down to up, to the comparative safety of the bivouac I had left. My mechanical ascenders wouldn't work on the icy rope; I tied special prusik knots so I could climb the rope. They held, but instead of sliding, they froze in place. My hands became immobile clubs, and I constantly fought blacking out as I neared the top. I yelled up to Warren to tie all our nylon loops together and lower them, but they reached only twenty feet. Dizziness overwhelmed me, and I didn't think I could make it. At long last I reached the loops and climbed the icy rope ladder to the Bat tents. They seemed much warmer—and Warren much smarter—than they had two hours earlier.

Hours later a faint yell from the base of the face signaled a radio call. For the first time in his life, Warren Harding asked for assistance: "We're not doing very well. We're wet, cold, and a little numb. Get us off if you can!" Our friends rushed down to the Valley and returned hours later with a terse message: "Helicopter...on... summit...two...hours." Then all was silent. Moisture had taken its toll on our cheap electronics.

Hours passed, and the sun set under a mantle of clouds. Suddenly a helicopter flew by, then made several passes. Our hopes soared, then dropped to a new low as the sky once more grew dark and silent. We knew that the helicopter couldn't fly near the cliff at night, so we concentrated on just surviving the agonizing cold. Long after dark we were startled by a strange, squawking noise. Then a light shone down the cliff, illuminating a man with a headlamp, radio, and heavy clothing being lowered on the end of a rope. Unseen by us, the helicopter had been shuttling people and equipment to the summit of Half Dome. The man on the rope was Royal Robbins, descending like a guardian angel to bring us hot soup, dry parkas and gloves, and a lifeline to the summit. We started to warm up as we climbed the 800-foot rope with jumar ascenders, and by midnight we were on top in a spacious tent with dry clothes, warm drinks, and old friends.

Four months later, in March 1969, Warren and I recovered our unique and expensive equipment by climbing the tourist route on the northeast side of the dome and then rappelling down to the Tri-clops Eye. We planned to give the face another go later that spring, but melting snow from the heaviest Sierra winter on record followed by Warren's commitment to a construction project kept us away. Warren notified his boss that he planned to take time off in September to resume our climb, but fate took another nasty turn. On the afternoon of his last day on the job, Warren's thoughts were thousands of feet above the central California highway project. He walked squarely into the path of a fast-moving truck, and his leg was crushed. For weeks the doctors didn't know if he would walk again, much less climb. But a series of operations reconnected ligaments and pinned shattered bones, and by December he was hobbling around on crutches and telling me: "May. We'll go back and do it this time."

Joe Faint had helped us recover our gear the previous winter, and he wanted to take part in the next attempt. On a sunny June day the three of us hiked to the base. I knew

Ponderosa pine below Bridalveil Falls, Yosemite Valley.

Warren was going to do fine when he limped past me with the heaviest pack. No sooner had we roped up for the first pitch, than the sky turned dark and ominous. It was our fourth storm in four attempts, and Joe began talking about omens. After our first bivouac, the weather was still threatening; and he suddenly wanted nothing more to do with the climb. We descended but were caught in a downpour before we reached the base. "Those who fail to heed the lessons of history are doomed to repeat them," Joe told us with finality. (We learned the next day that he was offering all his climbing equipment for sale.)

Several days later, on a clear morning, Warren and I returned. True to form, it began to snow before we had climbed the 400 feet of fixed rope back to our previous high point. With undiminished confidence—and plastic covers for our Bat tents—we resolved to wait out the weather. But as I stepped out of my tent to get some food from a haul bag, the sky lit up for a split second before the earth shook. The lightning gave me a strong jolt, sending me reeling against my anchor sling. Once I had recovered my wits, I figured out what had happened. When lightning strikes a cliff, electricity flows along cracks and flaws in the rock, and although we were on the least-flawed piece of rock in America, it did have one: the 900-foot crack in the arch that we were hanging from. The storm continued for two days. We tried to climb anyway, but got soaked in a small waterfall that crossed our route. On day three we descended.

On the first day of our sixth attempt, in July, yet another rainstorm hit us. It stopped as we continued to climb, however, and on the third day we reached our familiar high point in the Tri-clops Eye. The plastic water bottles we had filled in the Merced River four years earlier still dangled from the anchor bolts; we added purifier to the water and drank heartily. The weather stayed blessedly clear for two more days, as we climbed up a 200-foot blank headwall and into the thin cracks of the Gray Matter. On the third night's bivouac we hung our hammocks under a small overhang, not knowing whether we were one hundred or four hundred feet from the top.

Clouds moved across the sky all night long, and we awoke under total overcast at 5:30 A.M. I began a lead that consisted mainly of drilling and ended in blankness just before noon; then I broke out my Bat tent for the inevitable storm. I didn't want to think about the possibility that we might be forced down again, this close to the top. Raindrops fell as Warren donned his parka and started drilling up a black water streak that we had hoped might be a crack. The rock had a peculiar porcelain-like quality, as though it had been fired in a kiln, and was so hard that drilling took twice the normal time. For hour after hour the light drizzle threatened to worsen. I fed Warren all the rope, and he asked for more. Just as I gave him the last coil tied to my waist, he yelled, "Off belay! I'm up!"

As I climbed the rope to join Warren on the summit, a swift flew between us, unconcerned and unimpressed by our accomplishment. The fact that we had managed to falter our way through Half Dome's southern defenses had done little to change the formidable nature of the face. I remembered John Muir's words of exactly a century earlier, two years before a Scot named George Anderson drilled his way up the gentle slabs where cables now guide visitors: "The dome . . . would hardly be more 'conquered' or spoiled should man be added to her list of visitors. His louder screams and heavier scrambling would not stir a line of her countenance."

In this telephoto view of Yosemite, Half Dome appears to be next to El Capitan,
although in reality it is seven miles away.

# 4 / The Seventh Rifle

DAWN ARRIVED, but no sunrise accompanied it. A veil of autumn snow filtered from the sky, settling on the limbs of trees and on the blankets of the men who slept in the clearing. One man was awake, building a fire. Next to him, camouflaged by the white sky and falling snow, lay the fresh skin and feet of a mountain goat; nearby were the dim shapes of ten live horses and three dead grizzly bears. Under the trees lay an assortment of equipment, including a theodolite, several rifles, an immense camera, and an ice axe.

The year was 1910, and the setting was the Bugaboo Mountains of British Columbia. As I watched this imaginary scene out of the past, the sleeping men arose and joined their comrade by the fire. They talked of surveying and picture-taking, and of animals and shots they had missed with their rifles. They spoke of shooting at grouse, squirrels, deer, a bear cub. I wanted to jump in among them and say, "Look here! Have some respect for those animals! They have as much right to be here as you. And killing all those grizzlies—they're becoming scarce you know."

But this was sheer fancy, removed as I was by some sixty years and six thousand feet from that September morning scene. I was also pioneering, halfway up the 3300-foot face of North Howser Tower. My eyes were focused on a spot in a forested canyon more than a mile below me, and my gaze had not wavered for a long time. I wondered if I was looking at the spot where those men, the first Bugaboo climbers, had camped over half a century before.

At my back was a virgin granite wall; below me was some of the wildest country I had ever seen. In the whole vast panorama I could see no trace of a trail, a road, or other evidence of man, yet the image of that 1910 survey party intruded on my impression of an untouched wilderness. The current of evolution had been interrupted, however slightly, by early visitors with the pioneer ethic and lots of ammunition. More disturbing still was the realization that had I been alive in 1910 and sitting around the campfire with six men, ten horses, dead goats, grizzlies, and grouse, I would not have questioned their ethics. There would have been a seventh rifle leaning against the tree.

I started as though waking from a dream, but I had not been sleeping. It took me a moment to notice that the evening wind had blown out the camp stove at my side, and slowly I became conscious of the other details of my immediate surroundings. I was alone on a ledge, 1500 feet above a glacier. Above me, my climbing partners, Chris Jones and Tony Qamar, were fixing a rope. The ledge was strewn with equipment: bright blue sleeping bags, red jackets, orange jackets, various colors of polyethylene rain gear, freeze-dried food, jumar ascenders, a Bleuet stove cartridge, a bolt kit, and two ice axes. Except for the last item, how foreign it all would have seemed to Conrad Kain, the man by my daydream campfire.

The 1910 scene in the clearing I had recalled from a description in Kain's memoirs. The first mountaineer to explore the Bugaboo Range, he was also first to climb the

Alpine garden in the
Valley of the Ten Peaks,
Banff Park, Canada.

Camp under the west faces of the Howser Towers.

The 3300-foot west face of North Howser Tower, in the Bugaboo Mountains of British Columbia, rises from a glacier directly to the summit.

highest of the Howser Towers, the peak whose west face we were now climbing. If Kain were alive today, he would be in his late eighties, about as old as my father is. I could hardly believe that people of his generation, born in the age of muskets, before the advent of the automobile, were still alive in the age of the hydrogen bomb and space travel.

Our climb seemed to bridge that time span— it was technical in a limited sense, yet primitive—still wild, but only a long day's walk from civilization. We were carrying a bare minimum of equipment; if we succeeded, it would not be because we had carried all the "right" gear, as many advertisers would have one believe. On the contrary, it was the absence of items often considered essential that enabled us to move quickly in alpine rather than Himalayan style—climbing in one push without moving up and down fixed ropes between established camps on the face.

It felt satisfying to be doing a big wall in this "ethical" style. But climbing ethics are rarely as lofty as they seem. Often they are merely the ethics of convenience. For instance, British climbers began using nuts for protection, not because they saved the rock from damage—which has become the modern rationale—but because local rock was well-suited to them. Americans began to remove pitons en route not for montane esthetics but because they were heavy and costly. A climb like the Howser Tower might require ten pitons on each of thirty rope leads. This would mean carrying three hundred pitons that would weigh about seventy-five pounds and cost about $600. By recovering them as the last man came up, we were able to get by with a collection of only twenty pitons and a few nuts. On the low cliffs of England, or the less technically demanding climbs of the Alps, however, it made perfect sense for the first ascent party to leave its hardware in place. But now we were moving quickly and carrying as little gear as possible because heavy hauling is hard work; because the less time spent, the lower the odds of being caught by a storm; and because keeping my family in a motel in the nearest town was expensive.

Fixed ropes, placing bolts, and step-cutting in ice have all been called unethical by modern climbers. Doing without such techniques is indeed bolder, but it is also faster and less strenuous than the old-fashioned methods. Behind the mask of courage and style, the masters of modern techniques still follow the ethics of convenience.

Our three-man system moved us up the face efficiently, in much the same manner that the jerky, opposing motions inside an engine deliver a constant flow of power in one direction. Compared to the normal alternation of two climbers on a wall, our system allowed for only minimal rest time. After a lead was completed, the second climber jumared up immediately to take over the lead, while the third cleaned the hardware and tied on the loads to be hauled up. Pitch after pitch flashed by as we leapfrogged in this way over mixed terrain.

Bull elk (*Cervus canadensis*).

Chris Jones nears the top of the west face of
North Howser Tower during the first ascent.

Tony Qamar inside a great cleft
on the west face.

Chris kicked steps up a snow patch; I slithered over a wet overhang; Tony frisked past an awkward headwall. The holes in the knees of my 69¢ U. S. Air Force tropical blues gaped to the wind after a difficult jam crack. By lunch on the second day we couldn't count the pitches that we had climbed in the morning. As we nibbled on salami and cheese, a bald eagle glided past and landed on a rock gendarme. Without acknowledging our presence, the great bird soared on, then turned in a circle over the glacier and flew between our towers. An earlier generation might have taken that as an omen; as we watched the bird disappear, we thought of how it was an animal counterpart of a B-52 on a combat mission.

I began to gauge our progress by carving imaginary notches on the ridge of the adjoining South Tower. Following the ridge downward with my eyes until it ended on a snowy shelf, I spotted the black boulder under which forty man-days of food had been cached by an earlier expedition that had been forced off the face by bad weather. Having obtained their permission before our climb, we had feasted on canned bacon, hotcakes, and Trappist Monk brandy jelly—another benefit of coming sixty years after Conrad Kain.

As the sun set under a cloud bank, we traversed the final, knife-edged ridge to the summit. We bivouacked just below the top and found the morning air alarmingly warm. As we descended via the easier east face route, the bergschrund groaned repeatedly, and moments after I reached the glacier and stood clear of the steep wall, a wet snow avalanche erased my tracks behind me. Tony finished the last rappel and made new tracks rather more quickly.

After pulling out our camp at the base, we reached Boulder Camp, four miles from the roadhead, late in the afternoon. We experienced a strong dose of culture shock, for where generations of climbers had found only wildflowers and waterfalls, we were treated to the sight of two new huts erected by the Alpine Club of Canada—white plastic hemispheres capped with red ventilators. These dwellings housed a gaggle of guides, cooks, and clients on the main floor, and the basements were occupied by noisy families of super-ground squirrels. These rodents, termed "snafflehounds" because of their propensity for theft, had become a master race with a gene pool that changed far more rapidly than under natural conditions. The slow and unwary were shot with a guide's rifle as they free-climbed up the hardest boulders toward food or snaffle-prusiked up ropes toward suspended bags; in consequence, the survivors displayed considerably more speed, cunning, and wits that their primate cohabitants. To our dismay, we learned that the Alpine Club planned to move one of the huts to the west side of the Howser Towers, blasting a platform with dynamite if necessary. A newer, multistory hut would be built in Boulder Camp.

On a previous trip I had stayed in antique cabins at the roadhead. We now found them gone, and nearby the new Bugaboo Lodge graced a clearing below the toe of the glacier. The interior proved to be a tasteful blend of the Old World and the modern, yet I felt vaguely uneasy. I picked up a brochure bearing a picture of a helicopter hovering over the Bugaboos and the caption, "Conquer the High Country by Helicopter!" A

Sunrise on the Skeena River, British Columbia.

Walking across glaciers en route to North Howser Tower. In the background is Pigeon Spire.

sign innocently asked us to remove mountain boots before going upstairs, a ritual that defined our arrival in civilization.

My uneasiness gradually became fathomable. Had the Bugaboo Lodge been in town instead of near the foot of the glacier I would have welcomed its comforts with open arms. Now that the climb was over I had little desire to remain in the mountains. Kain had once stayed comfortable for months in the Bugaboo high country by carrying in enough equipment to live simply off the land. We had managed with far less gear while in the mountains, but always at hand was the prospect of a fast return to civilization. This was my "seventh rifle"—not actually leaning against a tree like Kain's but always part of my mental arsenal.

When Kain had returned from the Bugaboos six decades before, he hiked out thirty miles further to reach civilization and wrote in his diary: "It was pleasant to see a covered table once more and a good bed with sheets. But I could not sleep—it was too soft and comfortable."

Before the coming of winter, the stark landscape of the White Mountains
often looks like a scene from a Salvadore Dali painting.

# 5 / A Winter Traverse of the White Mountains

THE SOUND began as a low roar far up the canyon. Then it shrieked, groaned, and tore its way out of the sky as if a giant object were falling. Powerless, we braced ourselves for the inevitable shock. Out of the darkness it came: the headlong, invisible charge of the wind. Our tent leaned, twisted, stretched, and flapped, until it seemed no longer anchored to the ground. Then, suddenly, all was still again, except for the whisper of falling snow and the anxious, uneven breathing of the four men inside the tiny shelter.

For four days and five nights we sat out the biggest winter storm of 1974 in our camp at 10,000 feet in the White Mountains of California. Winds of more than 100 miles per hour, we learned later, had ripped the ice from the surface of a large lake twenty miles to the west. During a lull near the end of the storm, we skied to a grove of lodgepole pines in search of wood for a warming and drying fire. We found a healthy tree more than two feet in diameter that had been freshly broken—snapped off ten feet above the base. The broken piece, which must have weighed tons, had been carried thirty feet by the wind without leaving a single mark in the snow.

It was February 1974; the four of us were attempting the first winter traverse of the 80-mile-long crest of the White Mountains. Paralleling the Sierra on the east side of the Owens Valley, these arid mountains have few trees, no lakes, very few fishing streams, and a Great Basin climate, with recorded temperatures reaching as low as −38° F. Pellisier Flats, an 8-mile-long plateau at 13,000 feet, freezes every month of the year and has real arctic tundra. The crest of the range averages over 12,000 feet. Miles of treeless highlands are exposed to relentless west winds. During the Pleistocene epoch, these winds blew so much snow to the lee side of the crest that glaciers formed in cirques above what is now Nevada desert.

That same wind, not the steepness or the cold, was now our adversary. When we saw the storm coming on the fifth day of our trip, we descended toward timberline to about 10,000 feet. On the crest there was nowhere to hide from the relentless wind—no trees, caves, or natural windbreaks of any kind. At night our survival had depended totally on our four-man tent, which the manufacturer had personally assured us was the most wind-stable on the market. It was cozy inside, but from the outside, especially at night and with a light glowing from within, it seemed as fragile as a butterfly's wing. If the wind had ripped open a seam, we would have been rudely thrust into the arctic night.

As desolate as these mountains seemed, we were not alone. Although humans had yet to traverse the range in winter, we found surprising evidence of animals living at this unfriendly altitude. At 13,400 feet we had a rare encounter with a band of five desert bighorn sheep. At nearly 14,000 feet, tracks of coyotes and white-tailed jackrabbits made crazy, interlocking patterns in the snow. On a cache trip up a side canyon, one of us had seen a cougar at close range. And most surprising was a lone mustang standing on a bluff—at 10,000 feet in the middle of a blizzard.

Our foursome was a most unlikely group of adventurers; an ex-auto mechanic, two carpenters, and a sewer-line worker. Jay Jensen and George Miller, the two carpenters, lived in Bishop, California, a small town in the Owens Valley at the base of the White Mountains. Both had been introduced to wilderness adventures by Dave Sharp, the sewer-line worker, who had once been their high school teacher. Dave had an enviable winter job: making snow surveys on skis across roadless Sierra passes for the state of California. I was the ex-auto mechanic, and for me the Owens Valley had become a home-away-from-home. For many years while I still owned a business in the San Francisco Bay area, I frequently drove a thousand miles in one weekend to spend time there. However different our backgrounds, we all shared a deep attachment to exploring these desert peaks.

This trip climaxed many earlier visits to the White Mountains. George, Jay, and three friends had previously attempted a winter traverse of the crest in 1973. By the fifth day of that trip, they had covered less than a third of the total distance. Some eighteen inches of new snow had fallen, and they decided to dig a snow cave rather than risk pitching a tent in high wind at 13,200 feet. As usual in the Whites, they found the windblown snow very shallow; they were compelled to dig into a hillside and to build the cave on two levels with a low roof only two feet thick. At 3 A.M. Jay awoke with a sensation of being smothered. The roof was closer to his head than it had been; there was not enough light to see his hands in front of his eyes, and he began to feel panicky. The cave was starting to collapse. Quickly waking the others, he crawled outside into a 60-mile-an-hour wind and blizzard conditions. Putting up a tent was out of the question; some of the group couldn't even find their boots. Those who could locate theirs frantically dug a small alcove near the door of the cave, then tried to protect the entrance with the unfolded tent. Spindrift blew steadily inside; and gradually, over a twenty-minute period, the old part of the cave collapsed flat. The tiny alcove began to fill with snow.

A hungry coyote
(*canis latrans*)
out for a morning prowl.

Nearing the Patriarch Grove of bristlecone pines,
a place where earth and sky seem to meet.

Blindly, they fumbled into boots, gloves, and skis, and took off toward lower elevations. Within a few feet of the cave, George set off a small avalanche but luckily rode it out safely. A few hours later, on descending as far as a subsidiary ridgetop at 11,000 feet, they found clear weather; above them the crest was still in storm. The summits didn't come out of the clouds until fourteen days after they gave up.

The present trip had been planned more carefully. Realizing the seriousness of any equipment failure, we began with new, identical packs, gaiters, skis, bindings, and poles. The exception was George who insisted on trying thinner, lighter skis. A month before the trip, we had spent three days skiing up a side canyon to place a food cache on the crest. A second cache was flown in to the only permanent residence on the crest of the Whites, the University of California Barcroft Research Laboratory. At 12,470 feet, this facility is the highest year-round dwelling in the United States, supplied for more that half the year only by helicopter. Normally the lab discourages visitors, but we had obtained special permission to leave the cache.

But even careful planning can't anticipate the weather, and when the storm finally ended in its fourth day, we weren't sure how to proceed. The day before the storm began, we had reached the first cache and picked up a six-day supply of food; we now had two days' worth left. Some of us thought we should return to the cache—a full day's round trip—and pick up an extra margin of food for the 15-mile journey over the top of White Mountain Peak to the Barcroft lab. George suggested abandoning the effort altogether in favor of taking a ski run into Nevada, and then hitchhiking to a hot spring for a long soak. At last, however, we decided to go for it with only our less-than-ample provisions.

The morning after the storm ended was perfectly clear. In sub-zero temperatures we broke trail through deep snow; and by noon were back on the crest, enjoying the sun and the novelty of a rare windless day. Eye-to-eye with the peaks of the High Sierra across the 11,000-foot chasm of Owens Valley, we seemed to be far above the earth, skiing in the floating clouds. To the north, 150 miles away, we could see Mount Rose fading into the horizon. To the south, we looked past Mount Whitney to where the declining skyline of the Sierra merged with desert haze. Late in the day we arrived at a col at 13,400 feet. It was a strange place where some of the cornices, unlike those at our other camps, faced west instead of east. That evening we discovered why. Violent eddies of wind tried to rip the tent from its moorings, and we barely slept.

The next morning was still clear, and after an hour's skiing we reached the north ridge of White Mountain Peak—a granite knife-edge plastered with rime ice, with a drop of thousands of feet on either side. Tying our skis to our packs, we inched along the ridge through high winds and blowing snow, arriving at the summit around lunchtime. At 14,246 feet, White Mountain Peak was the highest point of our trip. The snow on the summit pyramid was glazed and wind-packed, and I was very glad to have metal edges on my skis for the steep run down the back side. The first mile went very quickly, but we soon reached an unskiable plateau where thousands of small rocks poked through the shallow snow. Barcroft Lab was still four long miles away. Some of us walked and others kept their skis on, stepping carefully through the rocks, trying to avoid the all-too-frequent grating noises. Late in the day, totally out of food and with the sky promising another storm, we finally reached the lab.

Our eleventh night in the mountains was very different from the first ten. We ate

A full moon
lights the crest
of the White Mountains.

steaks, took showers, and walked around in T-Shirts, perfectly warm. Upstairs in the two-story Quonset hut, we found the nation's highest library and its highest pool table, both in the same room. The library contained some rare nineteenth-century books on mountaineering and exploration. Reading them there, with the bitter cold blowing against the walls, lent a special significance to the historic adventures. The big storm that had trapped us in our tent had also damaged the power lines to the lab, and it was operating on emergency power from an ancient diesel generator. Mechanical failures were frequent; lights flickered, and the generator room took on the appearance of the hold of a leaking ship as hoses burst and workmen waded through a mixture of water and grease.

We spent two days waiting out the new storm: playing pool, reading, repairing ski bases, and watching the lab's resident mice and chickens. Its facilities were amazingly complete. Much high-altitude and space research has taken place in this tiny building which resembles an Antarctic outpost more than it does a California laboratory.

The next morning we were off again, stepping from the warmth of the lab onto snow that squeaked underfoot. For miles we followed treeless highlands, imperceptibly descending a thousand feet toward a gentle meeting with timberline. Not far from here a friend of mine had sat around a fire with a scientist named Edmund Schulman on a cool September evening in the 1950s. As the two men warmed their hands,

Twisted into concentric swirls by harsh weather over the millennia,
the limbs of this bristlecone pine connect to a still-living trunk.

Bristlecone pine,
the oldest known living thing.

Schulman pulled a brand from the fire and examined it closely. "1277 to 1283 A.D.," my friend recalls him saying. "This six-year ring pattern never repeats itself." When he had finished studying the flame-blackened ring pattern, he tossed the wood back into the fire. It burned long and hot and even.

Not long after that, Schulman became famous for his discovery that bristlecone pines are the oldest living things in the world. He never enjoyed his fame, however; he died before the publication of his most important work. History remembers Schulman as a practical scientist who proved with numbers and graphs that some bristlecones of the White Mountains are more than 4000 years old. My friend remembers Schulman as a man who lived in the wilderness of logic, seeking patterns in what appeared random—a man whose thoughts often wandered along loosely structured, mystical pathways. Already ill with heart disease in his forties, Schulman could not fail to note the contrast between the bristlecones and his own tenuous claim on life. He hoped to learn the secrets of long life from these trees, but, like Ponce de Leon, he never found his Fountain of Youth.

Even in his wildest dreams, however, Schulman never imagined the far-reaching effects of his discovery: that the twisted trees of the White Mountains would bring about a revolution in the study of Old World prehistory. Archaeologists formerly had dated Egyptian artifacts by accurate calendars left in tombs and European artifacts by the carbon-14 method; but Schulman's tree-ring chronology disagreed with carbon-14 datings of the wood—sometimes by as much as a thousand years. When the debate was finally settled, the bristlecones had won. A new bristlecone-corrected carbon-14 dating system came into being, which proved that artifacts of European culture were actually older than their supposed Mediterranean progenitors. The theory of cultural diffusion, which held that European culture was derived from the earlier civilizations of Egypt and Mesopotamia, was no longer valid.

Schulman had visited the bristlecones when the snow was gone and the trees rose naked from rocky ground. We saw them in quite a different setting, approaching on skis through an open forest clothed in white. The Patriarch Grove resembled a giant stage occupied by a troupe of frozen dancers; each tree seemed involved in the same motion, caught in pirouette, limbs extended. The relentless west wind had shaped them and coated them with fingers of ice. They seemed to point toward some distant force in the sky.

We camped on the edge of the grove, watching sunrise color ancient bristlecone limbs while a full moon touched the horizon of the distant Sierra. It seemed a sacrilege even to hang our sleeping bags to dry on those trees. Each of us ran his hands over their wood, feeling the sensual warmth of a living thing that was already old in the winters of 1492 and 1776. Compared to these trees, we were a renewable resource.

That evening, sixteen days after we had begun the traverse, we reached Westguard Pass at the south end of the range. Our thoughts were still on the heights as we returned to a much younger world in the valley below.

*70*

Twilight in the White Mountains.

Hetch Hetchy Valley, Yosemite National Park.

# 6 / *Yosemite's Other Valley*

THE TALE of Hetch Hetchy Valley resembles a Greek tragedy, but with a place instead of a person at its center. In the beginning there was a perfect half-scale version of Yosemite Valley, discovered by white men a year before they first entered Yosemite itself. While the larger valley soon bathed in international renown, Hetch Hetchy was being prepared for a different kind of bath. It was to become a reservoir. The final scene featured a star-studded cast that included John Muir, Woodrow Wilson, Gifford Pinchot, the Sierra Club, and most of the population of San Francisco.

As in all tragedies, the entire cast made out rather poorly in the end. Between President Wilson's signing of the fateful Raker Act, which permitted the long-fought Hetch Hetchy Dam to be built, and the actual drowning of the valley, both Wilson and Muir had died. Pinchot, undeniably a brilliant and conscientious man, would become infamous in environmental history for his support of a dam within a national park. Although Muir and the Sierra Club lost the battle, the city of San Francisco ended up with only half a plum: through a strange contract, Hetch Hetchy power is sold to the Pacific Gas and Electric Company before it reaches the city, and PG&E then delivers it to the consumer—at a huge profit.

Once the dam's work was done, Hetch Hetchy entered a kind of limbo. The promised recreational facilities never appeared on its steep shoreline, and for most of this century it seemed that the valley's sole use—other than for water and power—was as a propaganda tool against future wilderness encroachments. Countless old Sierra Club Annual Bulletins are sprinkled with references to the sad results of having sacrificed Hetch Hetchy:

"What is Hetch Hetchy now? Just another damned artificial lake."

"Hetch Hetchy now isn't worth a 35mm Kodachrome film."

". . . nothing but a narrow body of monotonous water with an ugly shoreline surrounded by stark stone walls."

"Why should anyone go to Hetch Hetchy now?"

Thus admonished, conservationists shunned Hetch Hetchy. Even climbers ignored the place, generally supposing that access to its superb walls was not possible without a boat. Since boats are not allowed on the reservoir, and since swimming with a load of climbing equipment is rather difficult, the "stark stone walls" remained untouched as late as 1969.

In the spring of that year Joe Faint and I made the first major rock climb in Hetch Hetchy: the 1400-foot face of Wapama Rock, the counterpart of Yosemite's El Capitan both in appearance and geographical situation. The approach to the face was a surprisingly pleasant two-mile trail that meandered along a wide glacial bench directly below the cliffs. The bench itself seemed little affected by human travel, and the ugly shoreline was not visible unless one walked to the edge of the bench and peered down. Over glacier-scoured granite, through streams, meadows, and wildflow-

Columbine lines a stream as spring comes to the Sierra Nevada.

ers, the trail delivered us to a point midway between two Yosemite-scale waterfalls. Two days later we reached the summit of the rock, but the main event of the climb was not this accomplishment; it was the change in our attitude toward Hetch Hetchy. We had started the climb with a feeling of who-cares-what-they've-done-to-the-valley-we're-just-going-to-climb-the-rocks; we finished it with a new sense of the meaning of wildness.

It began with a nightmare. We had bivouacked on a sidewalk-wide ledge about halfway up the rock ascent. Just before dawn I had been dreaming about sleeping on a ledge and slipping very close to the edge, but I wasn't worried because I was convinced that I was tied in. Then, still in the dream, I rolled over the edge, powerless to do anything but wait for the rope to stop me. It didn't, and I fell through the air for seconds—or perhaps minutes. I awoke with a start to find myself in reality very near the edge but reassuringly tight against the anchor rope. I peered through the pre-dawn haze at the imposing cliffs across the valley; still befuddled, I thought for a moment that I was on a climb in Yosemite Valley. It was the look down that turned my ideas about Hetch Hetchy onto a different track.

There lay the valley floor. But I saw no roads, no buildings, no campfires or smoke; heard no horns, motors, or voices. Below me was only a "narrow body of monotonous water" whereas if I had been in Yosemite Valley, the same site would have been occupied by Curry Village, fifty motor homes, a dozen tour buses, and the Valley tram car—all the dubious benefits of national park status. As the amber glow of the morning sun came creeping down the wall, we ate breakfast on our tiny ledge—a far cry from Yosemite Lodge, with its comfort, hot food, and Early Los Angeles decor. I repeated my environmental catechism: Yosemite was made a national park, and the Valley was saved for posterity; Hetch Hetchy was ruined for all time. It had a hollow ring.

In the spring of 1970 I returned to Hetch Hetchy, eager to repeat the serenely beautiful experience of the previous year. Joe Faint and Chris Jones joined me in an attempt to climb Hetch Hetchy Dome, a longer and smoother face than Wapama Rock. A full day of hard climbing gained us a huge ledge below the unbroken, 700-foot final monolith. Above the ledge the unforgiving glacier-burnished armor plate of the dome was punctuated by only a single system of vertical cracks.

In the morning we awoke to find gray masses of vapor moving past us with great speed. Below, the view of the reservoir flickered as we built a fire and discussed the merits of continuing the climb. Soon, falling snow brought about a prompt decision, and I suggested that the best escape would be to traverse eastward into a large gully. Although it dropped away toward the reservoir in a series of overhanging steps, the gully's upper half appeared to reach the rim of the valley without any obstructions. From the rim we could travel cross-country for several miles until we hit a dirt road leading to the dam.

An hour later we had completed a touchy roped traverse off the ledge and were walking up the gully through thick brush in a heavy snowfall. Several inches of snow covered the ground by the time we reached the rim of the valley, and visibility was less than a hundred feet. After crossing a raging stream, we crashed for hours through deadfall in a trailless forest, trying to convince ourselves that although we had no idea where we were at the moment, we definitely were not lost. Navigating by the moss on cedar trees, we attempted to follow a course parallel to the rim of the valley. We soon

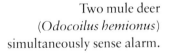

Two mule deer
(*Odocoilus hemionus*)
simultaneously sense alarm.

reached a place where the horizon was suddenly darker, and the wind seemed to be coming from below instead of in front of us. I threw a rock and counted eight before it hit with a splash; at least we now knew the location of the reservoir. After an hour's more hiking we reached the roadhead, resembling the survivors of Napoleon's retreat from Moscow and ready to embrace civilization.

Chris and I returned the following weekend, while Joe went climbing in Yosemite Valley instead. The intervening week had done nothing to lessen the difficulties of the lower section, and once again it took us a full day to reach the ledge at the end of the eleventh pitch. The fifth pitch is worth singling out. It followed a crack for a full one hundred fifty feet of consistent 5.8 and 5.9 climbing, with a 5.10 stretch at the finish. The lower half consists of a series of vertical lie-backs and hand-jams; the upper section is a continuous four-inch-wide crack, up which I wriggled with all the elegance of a dog chasing a cat through a storm drain.

Chris, who was not feeling well, relinquished the lead to me, and after what seemed like an eternity of exhausting direct-aid climbing, we finally reached the commodious ledge midway at day's end. The spot offered so many amenities—room to stretch our legs, a natural spring, firewood—that our night could hardly be called a bivouac. We barbecued steaks over a roaring fire and bedded down on soft ground.

In the middle of the night I was awakened suddenly; something was tugging at the down jacket under my head. I turned on the flashlight and saw a ringtailed cat calmly eating my Juicy Fruit gum—wrapper, foil and all. Ringtails are supposed to be shy animals, yet this fellow sat munching on my rations with the gall of an alley cat. As we stared at each other, the light from my flashlight reflecting in his eyes, I wondered which one of us was the intruder. I could perceive no fear in hs steady gaze but rather the calm assurance of a creature well in control of the situation. I began to resent his self-possession and looked around for something to throw at my uninvited guest. When I glanced back, he was gone into the night.

The ringtail cat (*Bassariscus astutus*) is among the most curious of North America's nocturnal mammals.

Chris Jones at the beginning of
the ramp on Hetch Hetchy Dome.

Before sunrise, Chris informed me that he felt much worse and might not be able to continue the climb. That he did choose, in the end, to go on showed an extraordinary amount of determination. Although Chris is not a strong free-climber, he has a long record of major ascents in mountain ranges all over the world, demonstrating that more complex factors are involved in making big climbs than merely the technical ability to lead the hardest pitches. I felt a heavy weight on my shoulders that clear, calm morning. Climbing with someone who is ill is as difficult as solo climbing, but has the additonal responsibility for another's welfare. I watched anxiously as Chris winced at the light from the sun as he followed a pendulum several leads above the ledge.

The climbing was mostly direct-aid in a single crack, which gradually dwindled into a water streak. Before it ran out, we reached a slanting horizontal ramp. With a bolt for protection, I face-climbed across the crackless ramp, feeling quite proud of my route-finding ability until I arrived at the end, where an unexpected blank headwall led to a marginal crack. By the end of the lead, I had placed two Bathooks, driven several shaky pitons, taken a short fall, skinned an elbow, and bruised an ego. Two bolts at the start of the next pitch gave me the confidence to free climb into a dihedral which led us to a ledge near the summit. Late in the afternoon we unroped at last and began walking up the inclined slabs to the crest of the dome. I felt happy and relieved; Chris was quiet and miserable. He was to spend the next week in bed recovering.

The walk back to our car provided a sharp contrast to our earlier retreat. Spring had arrived, and the greenness of life was everywhere. Only an occasional spot of snow in the shade of a log reminded us of the intense storm only a week before. Wildflowers carpeted clearings in the forest, and rivulets cascaded down every cliff. Hetch Hetchy had been trodden by people for more than a century, but on that afternoon we felt as though we had discovered it for the first time.

Ice hole in the Tuolumne River, High Sierra.

Moonset at sunrise over the crest of the High Sierra.

# 7 | The Moose's Tooth

TALKEETNA, ALASKA. Fifty-three residents, two airstrips, hundreds of dogs, and two bush pilots who refused to speak to each other. At ten in the morning the main street looked like a typical western town of the 1950s: two-lane road, dirt shoulders, neon yet to come. Outside the town bar sat two young men—one wearing Levi's, a sweatshirt, and a crewcut; the other in a Hell's Angel-style leather vest, cowboy hat, and gun belt. A wizened, almost-blind Indian, leaning heavily on his cane, rattled the door of the closed tavern. Age, alcohol, and twenty hours of Alaskan daylight had fogged his awareness of time. The bar did not open for many hours.

Two young men carrying rifles walked in lock-step in the main street, as a dusty Winnebago creaked over chuckholes not ten feet away. The driver of the Winnebago stared straight ahead at the pavement, ignoring the young men, who returned the compliment. The motorhome rumbled on another hundred yards to a dead end, where it turned around and headed back and out of town without stopping. Through the large, dusty windshield the motionless head of the driver seemed to form the pupil of a cyclopean, myopic eye, apparently unable to focus on anything but the road before it.

The true focus of the town was not the main street, however, but the dirt airstrip that led from the door of the tavern straight toward the river. A man dressed entirely in buckskin stood at the town end of the strip, negotiating with a pilot to airlift him with his dog team to a remote lake. He wanted a one-way fare; he had no plans for coming out. A prospector with tomorrow in his eyes approached me with a chunk of rusty metamorphic rock. "Gold," he said with evangelical emphasis. "It assays at over $200 a ton, but I've got to fly it out. I'd be rich if there was a road."

On the other side of the airstrip a chattering group of Japanese men wearing double boots and bright parkas busily crammed an enormous pile of equipment into a new Dodge van. In the distance, far beyond the town, beyond the river, and beyond the spruce forests, the Alaska Range loomed above the horizon. A forty-minute plane ride would soon transport us into an ice-age scenario. As if traveling through a fictional time warp, we would suddenly enter a Yosemite Valley of the Pleistocene, but one with a larger landscape and much higher rock walls, one where glaciers more than forty miles long plunged from alpine heights deep into wooded lowlands.

Our flight was delayed by a small oversight in logistics. Four of us—Jim McCarthy, Yvon Chouinard, Sandy Bill, and I—had come from different corners of the country to attempt the unclimbed 4500-foot granite face of the Moose's Tooth. Jim McCarthy had organized the expedition in New York. Since Yvon Chouinard owned a company that manufactured the best climbing hardware available, Jim had asked him to supply the expedition's pitons, carabiners, and chocks. Unfortunately, Jim's phone message failed to reach Yvon, so we met in Talkeetna with no equipment. It seemed that our climb might be over before it could start until Cliff Hudson, our bush pilot, located an expedition that had just returned from another technical climb. When he asked if they would loan their gear to an expedition that included Chouinard himself, they looked at their Chouinard equipment and had a good laugh.

Sunrise from midway up the southeast face of the Moose's Tooth, looking east down the Buckskin Glacier.

A 2500-foot granite pillar on the southwest side of the Moose's Tooth, climbed in 1974 for the first time.

Jim McCarthy was the leader in our obstinate quest to climb an Alaskan big wall. Although many snow and ice climbs of great difficulty had been made in the Alaska Range, none of its fabulous sheer cliffs had ever been climbed. A year earlier, in 1971, Jim had reached the 1800-foot level on the Moose's Tooth with Chris Bonington, Tom Frost, and Sandy Bill before a twenty-day storm drove the party back down. Only he and Sandy were returning. Sandy and Jim had also climbed together on the first ascent of the face of Lotus Flower Tower in Canada; they were well-matched for another go on the Moose's Tooth.

Chouinard, an incurable, grumbling romantic who had climbed a greater number of difficult alpine routes than any other American of his time, seemed at the moment to be going through a phase in which direct-aid climbing and long routes failed to hold his interest. While the rest of us discussed the Alaskan weather, Yvon kept talking about the surf in Southern California, but we hoped that once on the wall he would make the same remarkable effort that had gotten him up "impossible" faces all over the world. Yvon also gave us pause by asserting that a fast, light party could climb the Moose's Tooth in four days or less. Jim's idea of how to climb such a face was more conventional, and I concurred; I was terrified by the unknowns of Alaskan conditions. I wanted to bring hardhats, lots of wool, a fifteen-day supply of food, and waterproof hammocks—chiefly, I wanted to stay alive at all costs.

The morning after the equipment impasse was settled we flew up the Buckskin Glacier toward the Tooth. The toe of the glacier was covered with debris, but as we moved from temperate zones into the arctic world, its surface became pure white, broken only by crevasses and an unexpected set of animal tracks that led tens of miles beyond the last timber. Cliff explained that they were wolverine tracks, but he could think of no reason why the animal would venture up the glacier—except that wolverines are obstinate creatures. He glanced at us and smiled.

The Cessna 185 landed in a glacial cul-de-sac directly underneath the great cliff. We set up a base-camp tent and spent the night listening to avalanches crash around us.

Red fox (*Vulpes fulva*).

Across the cirque of the Buckskin Glacier, the southeast face of the Moose's Tooth rises for 4500 feet, sheer and still unclimbed. The 5000-foot face of Mount Dickey, on the opposite side of the Ruth Glacier, can be seen in the upper left of the photo.

A snowstorm blankets the granite of the Moose's Tooth.

The walls blocked out most of the sky in all directions; we had the impression that we were looking up from inside a well. We feared that without a view of the horizon, predicting the weather would be impossible.

The very next morning we began the climb on wet, decomposing rock. Forty feet up the first pitch a huge piece of ice was plastered to the cliff as though an oversized, half-cooked pancake had been thrown against it. Beyond the ice patch, a single crack, aiming for the sky, split the monolith. We had climbed for twelve hours when it began to storm, and we set up our first bivouac on small ledges a thousand feet above the base. All of us used hammocks except Yvon, who decided to test his company's newest rain gear by bivouacking on a ledge less than a foot wide.

The rain stopped just after dawn. Jim, Sandy, and I assembled together on a ledge about fifty feet above Yvon, who expounded excessively on the fact that he had stayed totally dry. I began free-climbing an intricate traverse that Tom Frost had figured out the previous year. Jim, who was to follow, had contracted a mild case of dysentery from bad water in the Yukon. All night he had held back his bowels until they developed the urgency and capacity of a ready-mix truck caught in a traffic jam; as soon as I left the ledge, he defecated onto a tattered parka left behind by the previous year's party. When it came time to follow my lead, Jim tied the parka in a knot and threw it off the wall. This unlovely package opened in mid-air, raining its contents on the hapless Yvon, who instantly regretted his decision to spend the night below us.

As Jim started climbing, he began to feel worse. His face took on a cadaverous hue, and he vomited uncontrollably. I expected him to voice doubt over his ability to make the final, unprotected traverse, but he said nothing; and I held my breath as he began a long, difficult diagonal up wet, rotten rock. He never faltered; his body had practiced hard face-climbing for so many years that he seemed to move by instinct. I never saw anyone move with such precision while feeling so poorly.

The quality of the rock continued to deteriorate as we climbed higher. On the first lead Yvon had used skyhooks on small flakes; by the fifteenth pitch I could remove any piton without a hammer and crumble the rock into gravel with my bare hands. Rockfall, too, became a serious problem. Missiles falling of their own accord from far above as well as rocks loosed by the leaders rained down on us. We all had brought hardhats except, as usual, Yvon, who claimed not to believe in them. After a particularly heavy barrage, however, he underwent a sudden religious conversion, and we began a ritual of reserving the three hardhats for the lower climbers. The unprotected leader was compelled to test his reflexes against the natural rockfall.

On the second evening we reached the first real bivouac spot on the wall, a sandy penthouse with accommodations for four. Although the ledge was wide, with enticing areas of level gravel that made perfect beds, that gravel could have come only from rockfall. If proof of the hazard were needed, two foam pads left behind during the previous attempt were almost completely covered by granite debris. I opted for another night in my hammock, in order to present as small a target as possible.

If our bivouac ledge was less than entirely safe, it had compensatory attractions. We were surrounded by bold beauty. In the distance was a perfect granite cirque capped with hanging ice. The monochromatic landscape of shades of gray was broken by a wreath of pink-and-green moss campion clinging to the face at the back of the ledge. It seemed magical that a single plant was able to survive in such harsh conditions. One pitch above the ledge we came upon a great sphere-shaped hole in the granite; inside were fist-sized crystals of quartz, tourmaline, and albite. We gathered a few loose ones and stuffed them into our packs.

In the morning Sandy and Yvon began leading above our high point. Jim waited on the ledge, still feeling under the weather but determined not to retreat. Sandy led a section of excellent rock; then Yvon encountered the worst rock of the climb—so crumbling that he had to begin drilling expansion bolts next to a rotten crack that wouldn't hold pitons. I could sense Yvon's frustration. He had finally hit his alpine stride and was eager to complete the route, but the terrain wouldn't permit him to advance. We watched him rappel down without completing the lead and, shivering in an icy rain that had just begun, we held a council of war.

Sandy thought the route should be pushed and was against going down, saying that he'd climbed through worse conditions in the Alps. Jim wanted to descend because of his illness. Yvon wanted to descend because the rock was so poor that he could not recommend the climb to anyone; *ergo*, it was not worth pursuing. I was developing the same symptoms of nausea and diarrhea that Jim had. I was willing to stay if the majority went that way, but my heart was no longer in the climb. The issue was soon decided: we descended.

The twenty rappels down to the glacier lasted well into the night. When the ordeal finally was over, we gazed up at what we had thought would be the Mona Lisa of the alpine world. From this distance she looked beautiful, but we had touched her flesh and found gangrene. Since that attempt six years ago, several other parties have tried the east face of the Moose's Tooth; each one convinced, as we were, that the reality of the face must surpass the descriptions brought back by previous expeditions. None have even reached our old high point. Perhaps they learned their lesson more quickly than we did. I went back to try the face a second time in May 1973, hoping that clear weather and freezing conditions would make the route feasible, but one flight past the face revealed it to be dangerously plastered with snow and hopelessly out of condition. I led the expedition to within six hundred feet of the summit by a route from the opposite side, only to be stopped by an overhanging wall of rock even more rotten than that on the east face.

"Granite," according to a British encyclopedia of mountaineering, "varies from place to place but is always sound to climb upon and a great favourite with climbers." We had learned that all things in the wilderness are relative; a granite face does not always offer superb climbing, any more than skill and training guarantee success. In a larger sense, though, our failure on the Moose's Tooth only enhanced the mysterious attraction of the place, and it firmed my resolve to return to the great walls of the Alaska Range.

Jim McCarthy on the first lead of the Moose's Tooth.

A wreath of life in a sterile world, moss campion
clings to the southeast face 2000 feet above the base.

Sunrise on Mount Whitney in July. Keeler Needle is the pointed peak
immediately to the left of the highest summit.

# 8 / *Free Climbing Keeler Needle*

IT WAS MY LEAD. I climbed thirty feet to the base of a smooth bulge where I stepped up and reached for a sloping handhold. My hand groped through loose gravel on the unseen shelf. Only ten feet separated me from easier going above, and I tried the same move again and again. No one had ever climbed those ten feet, and I realized then that neither would I.

I had been trying to bypass an overhang, and I was torn between two choices: relinquish the lead to Chris Vandiver, a better free climber than me, or attempt another way. I refused to consider a possible third choice: using direct aid placed in the rock to get past the difficult section. Why? Because three of us were attempting to free climb a rock face on Keeler Needle that had never been climbed without resorting to direct aid. It was just a game with us, but we were trying to play by the rules.

For decades the sport of rock climbing had been split into two factions: free climbers specialized in short, hard routes; big-wall climbers concentrated on long but technically easier routes. Wall climbs were traditionally approached with different equipment and ethics than shorter free climbs. In the past, climbers recognized the stylistic purity of the short climbs but considered free-climbing tactics impractical on the long walls.

Was it possible to break these conventions? We thought so. The overhanging east face of Washington Column in Yosemite had already been climbed entirely free. The Diamond, a big wall on 14,225-foot Longs Peak in Colorado, had also been free climbed recently for the first time. Chris Vandiver and I had done a free ascent of the west face of Mount Conness, the sheerest wall in the High Sierra, only two months before. After that ascent Chris had asked me if I thought Keeler would also "go free." I wasn't sure, having made the first winter ascent of the route with heavy equipment and liberal use of direct aid. But Chris's enthusiasm for the project proved infectious, not only to me but to Gordon Wiltsie, the talented High Sierra climber who in August 1976 became the third member of our mini-expedition.

Just two weeks earlier we had retreated from the same obstacle that was stopping us now: the tightest spot on this section of the rock tower, a slightly lower satellite of 14,496-foot Mount Whitney in the High Sierra. I had tried a different way, an overhang normally climbed with pitons for direct aid. I thought at the time about bypassing the overhang to the left, but it was too late on a cold and windy day. My fingers grew numb, the rock was rotten in critical places, and I got scared. We descended and spent that night below the face, hoping for warm, clear weather in the morning.

Dawn brought an incredible display of alpenglow, turning Keeler Needle's granite to gold. Every crack and rib was highlighted in bold relief. For several minutes we watched in awe until the colors suddenly disappeared. A hole in the clouds had closed, and the landscape took on the dismal gray of the sky. Our hopes for the climb wavered with the sunrise and were extinguished completely when snowflakes began to fall a few minutes later. We had no desire to attempt difficult free climbing during a snowstorm.

All that morning, while our gear remained one hundred fifty feet up the face, we lay in our sleeping bags biding our time until the weather improved. Voices wafted out of the mist from the east face of Mount Whitney, the cliff next to the Needle. Two climbers we had passed on the trail were up there in the storm. Heavily laden with pitons, hard hats, down parkas, and bulky mountain boots, they could survive many days on the mountain if the need arose.

When the storm showed no sign of abating by noon, we decided to go home and return in better weather. Chris waited in camp while Gordon and I headed toward the Needle to retrieve our equipment. An hour later, as the two of us were descending with the gear, we talked about the nearby east face of Mount Whitney. Gordon said, "I'd like to climb it some day; I've never done it before."

"How about now?" I hinted.

"You're kidding!" he replied. "It's 2:30 in the afternoon, and it's snowing."

"No," I said. "I'm serious. If we climb unroped we can be up and down in just a few hours. We can handle the difficulties, even in this weather."

Just then we heard voices above: the other climbers were still on the route eight hours after they had started. Gordon looked worried, no doubt expecting to be benighted on the peak, but his adventurous spirit won out. "Okay," he assented, "Let's try it." Chris declined to join us because he had just climbed another route on the same face. As we began the climb, Gordon experienced mixed emotions; he enjoyed the freedom of climbing unencumbered, but missed the safety of the rope. Both of us compensated for the lack of security by increased alertness. We checked and rechecked potentially loose rocks and placed our fingers and toes with far more conscious care than when backed up by the umbilical cord of a rope.

Just below the summit we caught up with the other two climbers, who were outfitted like models in a mountaineering catalog. Seeing that we were unroped, they asked if we had climbed to the top of Whitney by the horse trail and then had scrambled down for a look over the sheer face. When we answered no, they asked where and when we had started our climb. On learning that we had left the lake at the base of the climb only an hour and forty minutes before, they expressed amazement at the speed of our ascent. Actually, it was not so remarkable. The 1931 first-ascent party—four men wearing tennis shoes—had climbed Whitney's east face in three hours and fifteen minutes, unroped much of the way. Their leader was Robert L. M. Underhill, a famous figure in North American climbing history, who introduced technical rock techniques to both the Grand Tetons and the Sierra. In his account of that ascent Underhill predicted, "I believe a good climbing party that knew the route could ascend in something like half the time we required." By this standard, our ascent was three minutes slow.

Gordon was ecstatic when we reached the summit. We were able to relax; there was enough daylight left for us to descend to the road before dark, and, with no ropes or hardware to carry, the hike would be pleasant rather than laborious. In many ways, our spur-of-the-moment Whitney climb shared the same spirit as our plans for Keeler Needle. Although we would use ropes for safety on the Needle because of the greater difficulties involved, we would avoid engineering our way up the cliff. Our style would

Sunlight from below the horizon casts the jagged shape of the High Sierra crest onto the clouds.

Snow on the desert rocks east of the Sierra crest.

Warren Harding ascends
a fixed rope during the
1972 first winter ascent
of the east face of
Keeler Needle.

be more akin to that of Sierra climbers of the Thirties than to that of present-day big-wall climbers, and our accomplishment, if we succeeded, would mean more than just an isolated "first free ascent." This effort was part of a larger trend to merge the two disciplines of wall climbing and free climbing. For years each speciality had gone its own way, but we believed that the guiding principle of simplicity in mountaineering must eventually bring them together again.

Two weeks after our Whitney romp, Chris, Gordon, and I were back on Keeler Needle for another go. I climbed to the base of the overhang that had scared me on the first attempt and found that nothing had changed. The wall still swelled ominously overhead, and the single crack was filled with loose rock. My attitude, however, was different: I knew that I could not climb the only alternate route. After carefully planning my intended moves, I climbed six feet toward the overhang and came back down; then I repeated the sequence, wanting to memorize this section so I could save my strength for the more difficult area above.

After a long rest, I yelled down to Chris, "Okay, I'm going for it!" He fed out the safety rope as I climbed upward. I expected each move to stop me—to force me to try a different technique, or worse, to prove so difficult that I would fall—but a minute later the crux was over, and I was resting in a wide crack before the final, easier moves at the lip of the overhang.

Most good rock climbers could have climbed the overhang as I did, without resorting to direct aid. The hardest move was barely 5.10, a rating near the top of the scale of difficulty but today commonplace in most rock-climbing areas. The main reason no one previously had free climbed that section of Keeler Needle was that no one had approached the route as an ordinary rock climb. The east face of Keeler Needle had always been considered a "big wall," a multi-day climb requiring direct aid. Moreover, the face was an *alpine* wall where most climbers used gloves and stiff, heavy boots because of cold weather and snow.

Although we hadn't started until noon, we easily climbed more than half the face before dark. The absence of heavier equipment speeded our progress and enhanced the quality of the climb in countless subtle ways. I remembered one continuously difficult crack where I had used several direct-aid pitons in winter and watched with pleasure as Chris climbed the same pitch with hardly a break in motion. His thin shoes jammed perfectly in the narrow crack where earlier my mountain boots had grated on the outside edges. In spots where I had hung from pitons to rest, Chris stood comfortably with one foot jammed in the crack and the other on a tiny edge outside. He would climb ten or fifteen feet, pause to place a nut in the crack, attach it to his rope with a carabiner for safety, then climb another section.

We reached a bivouac ledge at sunset and prepared for the night as we had each done many times before. We strung a rope across the ledge and attached it to several anchors in the rock; then each of us tied himself in. Darkness came quickly, but sleep eluded us for hours. We talked about climbs and friends we had in common; and when we tired of that, we gazed silently at the lights in the town of Lone Pine, fifteen air miles and 10,000 feet below our airy perch. We felt far removed from the world of hot sagebrush plains and civilization. Our own world was condensed into some nine hundred feet of granite, the distance between us and the summit.

In the cool, clear dawn, Chris, Gordon, and I sat huddled together, waiting for the sun's warmth to flow into us before we resumed climbing. After a cold breakfast, we packed all our gear into two medium-sized packs—quite a departure from most big-wall climbs where equipment must be laboriously hauled in huge bags up the wall. I felt almost guilty that the climb had required so little effort thus far. Spared both the drudgery of hauling heavy loads and the tedious work of hammering out long rows of direct-aid pitons, we were free to absorb the great beauty of Keeler Needle's setting. We were limited only by the extent of our skills rather than by logistical complexities.

Our test of those skills came very soon. I led an easy pitch to the base of a long corner. The next lead was Chris's, whose talent as a free climber is almost over-shadowed by his exceptional control in tight situations. Because his movements are consistently smooth, many people who have seen him climb have found it impossible to tell where the real difficulties lie. I had climbed with him often and knew the telltale signs.

Aspens in Mill Creek Canyon, east side of the Sierra.

The High Sierra in June. Mount Whitney is visible in the extreme background at the left of the photo.

Chris climbed the first forty feet of the corner with long, fluid motions, stopping occasionally to place a nut in the crack for safety. Reaching a spot where the crack was about six inches wide and overhanging, he found a row of expansion bolts on the wall next to the crack, marking where previous parties had ascended rope ladders clipped to the bolts. Chris wriggled halfway into the crack, which was too narrow for his chest and too wide for a fist- or knee-jam. At low elevations many climbers vigorously wriggle up such cracks, but to do so at 14,000 feet would almost certainly result in fatigue and a fall. Chris reduced his efforts to tiny movements that gained him only an inch at a time. His eyes brightened, and his expression grew intense as he used all his skill to keep from sliding out of the crack.

I watched him from the ledge below. Although his movements looked less spectacular than on many of the easier pitches we had already climbed, I knew that this impression was deceptive. Chris was making an incredible effort, but it was taking place inside—in the interaction of mind and body. Only he knew how closely he was approaching his limits.

Chris gained a large foothold and took a long rest; and when he resumed climbing, his movements once again were easy and graceful. Although the greatest difficulties were over, we weren't yet sure that the climb was in the bag. I couldn't remember every move from my last climb, but I did recall a long section of direct aid quite near the top. Throughout the rest of the morning the three of us alternated leads up the face, encountering only moderate difficulties. When we reached the place where I had used direct aid on my winter ascent, we saw an obvious bypass to the difficulties: a system of

97

California gulls (*Larus californicus*) nest east of the Sierra in alkaline lakes that are remnants of the inland seas their ancestors once inhabited.

cracks that in winter had been plastered with snow and unusable. Now, however, Chris quickly traversed to the very prow of the Needle where an absurdly positioned ledge interrupted a curtain of granite that dropped in a single sweep. It looked like a window-washer's scaffold on the side of a skyscraper.

The difficulties were nearly over; even in winter we had free climbed most of the route above. The final pitches went quickly, and shortly after noon we reached the summit. It was, as always, a satisfying moment, but far more satisfying was the knowledge that we had accomplished our goal of climbing the big wall without big-wall techniques. We lingered only a few moments, then coiled our ropes, stuffed them into our packs, and descended a few hundred feet to a trail, where we merged unnoticed with the queue of weekend hikers heading for the summit of Mount Whitney.

From the summit we dropped down a gully into the mountain's afternoon shadow. Most shadows move as slowly as the hands of a clock, but Whitney's shadow chased us through the timberline paradise faster than we could scramble. It skimmed down cliff bands and boulders, slowing only for level sections of meadow and forest, until, like us, it traveled across the hot desert floor toward town.

# 9 / Skiing the High Desert

THE GREAT BASIN extends from the crest of California's Sierra Nevada to the Rocky Mountains; it was so named by explorer John C. Fremont because it has no drainage to the sea. All waters in this vast region eventually run into alkaline "sinks" in the desert. Astronauts have reported that from outer space the Great Basin looks like a brown field sprinkled with giant caterpillars crawling south. The caterpillars are desert mountain ranges, more than fifty of which reach over 9000 feet in elevation. They are roughly parallel and separated from each other by flat, arid valleys. The view from the highest summits is a repeating sequence of distant ranges and valleys. It is like being in a giant room with mirrors on two facing walls: the images on both sides are similar and ever more distant.

Summer backpackers find these desert mountains hot, dry, and brown. Forests are sparse, lakes almost nonexistent, and fishing streams few and far between. Desert hikers usually head east or south of the Great Basin into the shaded, well-watered canyons of the Colorado River and its tributaries. In winter, however, the Great Basin ranges become more like their alpine cousins. Their rounded crests become corniced ridges, and the sage blanket of the lower slopes disappears beneath snow. Temperatures often drop below zero; Jiggs, Nevada, below the Ruby Mountains, once recorded −55° F. The snow-covered desert ranges differ from the Rockies and the Sierra mainly in their long, open sections, exposed to the elements and unbroken by trees, cliffs, or shelter of any kind. It is this aspect that makes winter travel in the Great Basin a more serious undertaking than in the more alpine ranges of the United States.

After successfully traversing the crest of the White Mountains in 1974, I looked forward to another Great Basin ski adventure. A member of that trip, Dave Sharp, interested me in his home mountains, the Ruby Range, one of the largest in Nevada. Eventually, a total of eight people wanted to ski the 100-mile crest, so we split into two separate parties of four. We planned to meet in the mountains and travel together where feasible.

Early in the winter we skied up two side canyons and placed caches of food and fuel. Then we learned that Dave would be unable to join us for the final traverse. In his place we asked Mike Farrell, an experienced skier and climber, to join us. My group also included Doug Robinson, the first person to continuously ski the entire length of the John Muir Trail along the Sierra Crest, and Dave Lomba, a recent convert from the downhill slopes. George Miller organized the other foursome, which was composed of friends from eastern California.

In early March we returned to the Rubies and began skiing from Overland Pass at the south end of the range. On the first night we camped with George's group in the pinyon pine belt just above the open sagebrush at 6000 feet. For several days thereafter, we plodded through snowstorms. Forests became mystical places where somber forms suddenly materialized from the mist like headlights out of a fog, and the bristlecone pines seemed like pagan idols brooding over the inhabited valleys below.

The Ruby Mountains of Nevada from the east.

These contorted trees were fluted with rime ice that perfectly complemented their overall configuration—little wonder, since the same wind patterns that sculpted the ice had shaped the bristlecones over the course of thousands of years.

The previous winter, in another Great Basin range, Dave Lomba and I had tracked down the oldest living bristlecone ever discovered, a tree that had died in 1964—sacrificed to the cause of research. The story of its death had been hushed up; only by reading between the lines in scientific journals did it become apparent that a 4900-year-old tree with living branches had been felled and then sectioned with a chainsaw. At dawn on a March morning we found the tree's remains on a moraine at 10,750 feet below Wheeler Peak, the highest mountain wholly in Nevada.

Trees that have died natural deaths are often more beautiful than living ones, and I couldn't pass these ancient souls without being reminded of the words my mother had written when I was a child:

> The grandeur of Death in Nature! To see a tree that has lived and covered itself with foliage finally die, and for the first time show the Strength and Line of its limbs. To raise them naked and unashamed from the earth to the sky and there, silhouetted, to create for the whole world Beauty as it never before has been conceived.

I found death by the hand of man an entirely different matter. A stump protruded from a blanket of winter snow, and chunks of chainsawed wood lay in the snow like arms and legs on a battlefield. The Forest Service had granted geographer Donald Currey permission to cut down a tree in order to date Little Ice Age events. Currey used a special drill to remove a pencil-sized core from a tree more than 4000 years old. He missed the center of the tree, so he tried again. The tool broke off. Rather than wait months for a replacement, he asked that the tree be sawed into sections. In his scientific report Currey offers no apology for the destruction of the earth's oldest known living resident, which he fondly calls WPN-114.

After Currey's "discovery," the Forest Service invited a team of dendrochronologists to search for a still older tree. But WPN-114 was an anomaly; no bristlecone in that region was discovered within 1200 years of its age. Today the oldest living thing by default is the Methuselah Tree in the White Mountains; its exact location is kept a secret for fear that tourists will desecrate it or carry off souvenirs.

Bristlecone rarely die in natural catastrophes. With the exception of an occasional lightning strike they grow too high and too far apart for fire to kill them. A few have toppled after gradual erosion of the mountain surface around them exposed their roots. Large trunks with bark on them lie at the bottoms of the steepest canyons in the White Mountains, apparent avalanche victims of the colossal winter of 1969. But the bristlecone's only real threat is from modern man; and in the twenty-odd years since humans "discovered" the tree, they have wreaked more damage than the previous 2000 years. The cool, clear wind that brightened Schulman's campfire in the 1950s now carries measurable air pollutants. Some of the oldest snags are gone, in the interest of science—and wood paneling. Others have found their way into campfires, wood stoves, and curio shops. Their very longevity makes them especially vulnerable to human impact. With growth rates often less than an inch in diameter per century, they cannot recover quickly from damage, as rabbits or eucalyptus can. Their survival—and ours as well—depends on slowing down the frantic scramble we call civilization.

In the Ruby Mountains we found bristlecones far more intact than those I had seen near roads in the White Mountains or near the sectioned tree on Wheeler Peak. Day after day in this harsh, untracked landscape we grew closer to the timeless world of the trees. One day of storm and drifting snow blended into the next. We forgot about

*The ex-Oldest Living Thing on Earth*
*Was ancient when Cortez conquered Mexico—*
*Was bent with years when Caesar entered Gaul—*
*Was old beyond memory when Moses delivered the Law—*
*Was Time's patient watchman when Cheops built his pyramid—*
*Was sliced by a chainsaw to see how old it was.*
Requiescat in Pacem.

Bristlecone #WPN-114, Wheeler Peak, Nevada.

sunlight. Our world was always gray and timeless. It was only winter, and there was only snow. Night arrived like a morning fog, softly and unannounced.

One morning a week into the trip, the storm was too heavy for traveling. By midday it abated, however, so all eight of us decided to ski down a bowl on the west side of Pearl Peak. It was absolutely fantastic: two to three feet of light powder lay on top of many feet of settled snow. Unencumbered by our packs, we floated silently down through open bristlecone forests, lost in the splendor of a white world with no firm boundaries between earth, air, and sky. Here was wilderness skiing at its finest—superb conditions, as good as the best of Alta or Aspen, in a paradise where no one had ever skied before. I thoroughly tired myself by making six 1000-foot runs through the powder, each followed by an hour's climb back to the crest.

The next day we looked forward to a descent of nearly 3500 feet from the top of Pearl Peak, but the view from the summit proved disappointing. The slopes were extremely steep, and the avalanche danger was too acute for skiing. We chose instead to climb down a long rock ridge, carrying our skis on our packs. As we descended, the snow lost its fine powder consistency, and minutes after we again put on our skis, Dave Lomba's binding pulled out of his ski, a mishap that had already occurred once before. Taping it temporarily to the ski, we continued down to an abandoned Basque sheepherder's cabin in an aspen grove by Smith Creek at 7000 feet to make more permanent repairs. We fired up the old wood stove to keep the room warm enough for the epoxy to set.

The next morning we were back on the trail, half a day behind George's group. The canyon bottom was serene, in sharp contrast to the harsh world of the crest. Gone

*Left:* Limber pines and snow soften the contours of a rugged land. Lamoille Canyon, Ruby Mountains.

*Right:* Descending through a limber pine forest in Nevada's Ruby Mountains.

Bristlecone snag below Wheeler Peak, eastern Nevada.

Drying gear after a storm
on the crest of the
Ruby Mountains.

were the twisted pines, sandblasted by the wind-driven snow and sculpted by a west wind that was already blowing when men still lived in caves. Here the trees were hardwoods—aspen and mahogany—and the sun-molded spring snow gleamed like porcelain.

Two days later we climbed over the crest again in rare clear weather. On the other side a steep glacial cirque with open, high-angled slopes dropped to a frozen lake. In the hour it took to reach the lake, the weather had changed again. A storm seemed imminent. We found an old cabin built of roughly hewn pine logs at the edge of the lake, and although it had no windows and was totally dark with the door closed, it seemed a more desirable shelter than our flapping tent, especially if the weather worsened during the night. Making it habitable proved to be more of a project than we anticipated, since it was filled nearly to the roof with snow. We spent hours digging it out, then chinked the holes in the roof and walls with blocks of snow and prepared for the night.

I awoke at midnight to the call of nature and ventured outside in sixty-mile-per-hour winds. The sky was cloudless, but the stars were dull, as though seen through a dusty window. By morning a real blizzard was in progress, and we quickly discovered how the cabin had filled with snow. Spindrift leaked rapidly through the timbers, covering us and all of our belongings. To add to our discomfort the temperature was well below zero; I spent the dark day inside my sleeping bag wearing all my clothes and my down parka. We wondered how far ahead the other foursome might be and where they were camped during the blizzard, but we needn't have worried—unbeknownst to us, they had given up on the tenth day of the storm.

I felt like a human subject in a deprivation experiment. I'm the type that always has to be doing something, even if it's just scribbling or pacing the floor; but here there was absolutely nothing to do. For two days and three nights I couldn't read, write, or see the outside world. After two restless nights I realized how differently Doug Robinson experienced winter. He didn't think in terms of days of the week, hours of the day, or degrees of temperature. He was totally in tune with the wilderness of snow and sky:

Sunrise on Pearl Peak,
Ruby Mountains.

seeing without categorizing, traveling without scheduling, discovering without searching. He created another world for himself, one separate from ordinary reality. Only equipment tied him directly to the world he left behind. Like Tolkien's Frodo, his life was an unhurried journey toward distant rewards.

Our stay in the cabin finally ended on the twelfth morning of the trip; and it was windless, cold, and clear as we set off. Only ten minutes out, Dave ripped off his binding yet again. We spent an hour on a makeshift repair, hoping that we could continue along the crest for at least a few more days. But meanwhile the sky had clouded over, and strong winds created a ground blizzard. After a council of war, we decided to retreat.

The descent through a trailless, brushy canyon was an exhausting, all-day affair. Late in the afternoon we struck a dirt road and followed it to a modern ranchhouse. An old rancher came to the door and broke into loud guffaws of laughter; he had never seen anything like us before. Later we heard that his wife had spotted us walking up the road—colorful, muddy, and bedraggled—and when she had called her husband to the window, he had asked her in all seriousness, "Are them Indians?" We were treated to some gracious Western hospitality, and then the old rancher had his son drive us forty miles back to our car, where another surprise awaited us. The car had been burglarized of all our personal belongings, more than $1000 worth of everything from handmade equipment to underwear and tire chains. "Must have been those city people," said the rancher's son.

The sheriff's office was in a town nearly a hundred miles away. "Must have been some locals in the valley. Probably Indians," we were told there.

Although we had lost some of our most treasured possessions and had failed to travel the full crest of the Rubies, these misfortunes could not break the spell that the high desert had cast. On the way home, we were already planning to traverse another lonely crest the following winter. As we drove west for hundreds of miles along Highway 50, snowy ranges rose before us. Here, so close to civilization, was an unofficial wilderness that remained virtually unexplored in winter.

# 10 | A Vertical Mile in the Alaska Range

THE INTERIOR OF the Alaska Range is an alpine world few people realize exists on earth: ice, rock, snow, and sky, each element in oceanic, overpowering quantities. Unlike the Himalayas, the landscape is nearly monochromatic. There are no greens, and yellows and reds appear only at sunrise or sunset. The scene is white, gray, and blue.

The giant rhythms of this land distort normal perceptions, and thoughts slow down like records played at too slow a speed. We humans have natural clocks, reset each day by sunrise and sunset, high noon and stars. But June in the Alaska Range has twenty-hour days followed by brief, starless twilights. Near the solstice, weather permitting, the sun shines all day on the summit ramparts of Mount McKinley, whose 20,320-foot bulk intercepts light beams aimed at the arctic circle nearly 200 miles north. McKinley's shadow scribes a daily arc over thousands of miles of primeval landscape.

Well informed as we are about travel to the moon and planets, most of us know little of this ice-locked part of our own nation. In 1903 Frederick Cook followed the great shadow's arc around Mount McKinley in a 540-mile orbital expedition that has never been repeated. Three years later he was the first person to travel up the Ruth Glacier (named after his daughter) en route to an attempted ascent of McKinley. He discovered the Great Gorge, where some of the greatest granite faces in this hemisphere tower over either side of the glacier. True to the giant rhythms of the area, distances and features are much greater than they appear.

Until 1974 not one face in the Great Gorge had been climbed, and in the summer of that year I came to Alaska with Dave Roberts and Ed Ward to attempt the southeast face of Mount Dickey—the highest granite cliff in North America. The peak has a moderate snow and ice route up the back side, but drops a vertical mile to the Ruth Glacier and an unknown distance below the surface of the ice. The three of us had been on a combined total of more than twenty expeditions to the North, but our first sight of Dickey from the air still took our breath away.

As we were flown into the gorge by the legendary bush pilot Don Sheldon, days of foot travel were compressed into minutes of flight. Sheldon edged his supercharged Cessna 180 close to the wall for a look at our proposed route. Snow-covered ledges tiered like the windows of a high-rise building inspired both confidence, as resting places, and apprehension, as potential traps during a long storm. The area has received more than eighty feet of snowfall in a single season. Much of the snow on those ledges had only recently been salt water in the Gulf of Alaska, perhaps lapping the sides of a Japanese fishing boat or roaring up Cook Inlet with the tide. Although we were now a mere stone's throw from the ledges, they were actually a hard week's work away.

We landed at Sheldon's "Mountain House," a tiny cabin he had built on a rock promontory on the Ruth Glacier to accommodate his clients. It was the only building for fifty miles around. At 2 A.M. the next morning we set off to climb Mount Dickey by

Aerial view of the upper southeast face of Mount Dickey. The climbing route lies just to the right of the left skyline.

the easiest, north side in order to cache a tent, food, and ice axes on the summit. At one point an invisible snow bridge collapsed, and I fell into a gaping hole. The rope snapped tight just as my skis struck a snow shelf inside the crevasse. Unhurt, I stared thirty feet overhead to the hole in the roof of the icy trap; by luck I had missed hitting hard ice nearby. Using mechanical ascenders, I escaped on a rope that Dave and Ed anchored above, and we continued the climb. The weather gradually enclosed us as we approached the summit ridge. We cached our supplies and descended by the same route to a col, marking our route with willow wands tagged with red ribbons. We camped on the col that night, then continued around the mountain to a base camp at the foot of the southeast face, where we waited through several days of poor weather to begin our ascent of the wall.

There was only one natural campsite on the vast glacier, a Shangri-la in the relentless, icy world. Base Camp was secure and friendly—warm clothes, level glacier, no bugs, no rockfall, no avalanche danger, plenty of food, and books to read. Boulders and gravel lay strewn on the ice, the beginnings of a lateral moraine. A flat, ten-foot rock was our kitchen, and a stream flowed into a deep blue pool nearby.

Our strategy was completely different than it had been on the Moose's Tooth two years before. Instead of bringing vast amounts of equipment and food in order to survive storms en route, we planned to go light and rush the face when a break in the weather came. To get a slight head start we spent a preliminary day fixing four ropes on the lower part of the face. The rock was firm, and the weather was as balmy as summer in the Tetons. Dave later wrote, "If we got no higher than this... we'd have had one great day of climbing, the like of which whole expeditions starve themselves for in the Alaska Range."

We planned to climb with only a three-day supply of rations—and no tent. We would have to move through the mountain's defenses for up to eighteen hours a day, quickly, decisively—a problem not unlike that of crossing a freeway on foot on a dark night. Better naked and fleet of foot than the deceptive safety of plodding caution.

After waiting out a short storm, we began the ascent beneath clearing skies on July 17 at 2 A.M. It was still early in the morning when we reached our previous high point at the top of the fixed ropes. The loads were the lightest I'd ever taken on a big climb, even back home in California. Relying on the snow, we carried little water. I had two wool sweaters and a rain parka—but no down jacket. We carried one tarp, one bivouac sack, one ice axe, and a single pair of crampons—token gestures if conditions became extreme.

On the huge, complex cliff we felt like rats in a vertical maze. Each lead was a pathway which had to connect with the next in order for us to get through. Because we moved separately and concentrated intensely, our inward experiences were rarely shared. Dave would slow down on an unpredicted section of rotten rock, but neither Ed nor I would really ever know how bad it was. We'd see it as we mechanically ascended the rope after him.

"Nice lead, Dave."

"Thanks."

Then I'd watch Ed lead higher, back on firm rock, moving confidently and using nuts and occasional pitons for safety. His hour of hard work, too, would rush by me in five minutes as I climbed the rope to take the lead above. Our progress was relatively

The thirty-eight-mile-long Ruth Glacier
from midway up Mount Dickey.

rapid, about one hundred feet per hour. In other parts of the world this would work out to six nine-hour days of climbing to ascend the mile-high wall. But we had started at 800 feet, and we hoped to climb for eighteen-hour days. Light gear, long days, and a little luck would put us on the summit in three days, in theory.

On the twentieth lead, about 2000 feet above the glacier, our mechanical ritual was halted by a series of problems. The rock was rotten and frostriven. A section of the wall that had appeared relatively gently angled now proved desperately dangerous. Higher, a vertical headwall of crumbly rock was broken only by a single flaw, a wide chimney hundreds of feet high. It was my lead, and using a rope traverse, I entered the chimney and found firm rock inside. Its sides were slick with water, however, and its few ledges covered by snow. My progress was blocked by giant chockstones, one of which required 5.9 climbing—close to the upper limit of difficulty on dry firm rock. The chockstone thrust outward like an awning, dripping water on my head. Jamming hands in the wet crack that connected it to the wall, I worked my way to the outside edge, reaching blindly over its brow into gravel and snow. A fall seemed certain so I backed down to a resting spot and then tried again, this time driving a piton into the crack near the lip. This would at least protect me from a long fall, and I moved upward more confidently, frictioning my boots against the flaring walls of the chimney. They held, and I soon had a death grip on a blocky handhold. At the end of the lead I reached a ledge. The absolute clarity of my mini-battle with the chockstone soon diffused into dull anxiety about our progress.

Later that evening, Ed completed a difficult pitch in the ten-o'clock twilight, and we bivouacked on a comfortable ledge. We cooked dinner and talked optimistically about our progress: half the climb completed in a single day, with, of course, a head start of fixed lines. Soon we were dozing beneath the clear sky.

The sunrise poured through slots in thick clouds to spotlight summits with an eerie orange phosphorescence. Yesterday we'd seen only occasional cirrus clouds moving from the south like a giant migration of geese, but today a storm was upon us. Valleys to the south were locked in cloud, and streamers of white mist crept up the Ruth Glacier, lapping at the base of our mountain like the breath of an unseen dragon. In the gloom of four-o'clock dawn we discussed whether to abandon the climb. Our decision to keep moving up was made out of psychological commitment, not logic.

There was a world of difference between the first and second day's climbing. The vastness was suddenly gone, replaced by dank confinement. Gone were the ice highways twisting through distant gorges. The sky was depthless gray, as was the air below our feet; clouds below me made the rope disappear. At noon we reached an amphitheater surrounded by overhanging rotten walls and again found the rock bad—so bad I could chop steps in it with my alpine hammer. The only way out was to climb the skyline to the right. Dave led to a ledge beneath a steep headwall. On the next lead, he mistook my call for "slack" to be a warning of "rock!" and instead of feeding the rope, he pinned me for life's longest seconds on rotten rock high above a dubious safety anchor before he finally understood my yell. We had no confidence that either pitons or nuts could safely anchor the rope in such poor rock. Imagine a floor covered with marbles. Make the pile of marbles bottomless, glue them together in some weak fashion, tilt the angle to sixty degrees, and you have a rough approximation of the difficulties. Even in chopped steps my feet felt insecure. It took me more than two

Ed Ward high on Mount Dickey. Visible in the background are the cliffs of the Moose's Tooth.

hours to climb a hundred feet up terrain that I knew I couldn't climb down. Finally I reached a ledge—a triumph but also a trap, for the cliff above was vertical and blank.

I had the dull feeling that we'd done something irreversibly wrong, but Ed had a perpetual smile on his face; I feared he didn't understand the gravity of our situation. But Dave's notes on the climb contained a similar appraisal of me: "Would Galen... keep that blithe cheerful countenance to the end?" I began to understand why politicians smile.

Ed was still smiling as I lowered him around a blind corner, to search out a route in the invisible gloom. His voice, now more cheerful than his face, warmed our hearts. "Perfect rock. It goes!"

Throughout the climb we could find no reason why the rock was good in some places and bad in others. We knew that the bad rock was shattered by exposure to the elements, but the good rock was the same quartz monzonite and good and bad were often found side by side on similar exposures. The good rock was climbable even when it was overhanging; the bad rock was virtually impossible as it approached the vertical.

Sun halo over Mount Dickey
at the beginning of a storm.

The 5000-foot wall of Mount Dickey crowns the Great Gorge of the
Ruth Glacier—an Alaskan Yosemite still locked in Pleistocene ice.

We were lucky to have escaped the amphitheater before the storm began. A few hours' delay and the rock would have been plastered with snow. We climbed all afternoon on fine rock, wondering when the storm would begin and hoping that its slowness was not an indication of its size. By early evening it had begun raining, and we stopped on a giant ledge about 1000 feet below the summit.

The rain turned to snow, and a strong wind came up. An Alaskan blizzard was upon us. Dave covered himself with the tarp and slept in a small nook; Ed crawled into the bivouac sack and remained exposed on the ledge. Blanketed with snow and curled in fetal position, he looked, Dave said, "like a victim's body discovered by rescuers." I wriggled into a natural coffin under a boulder. Protected from the wind, but exposed to blowing snow, I spent the night so cramped that had the rock shifted half an inch I would not have gotten out. Sleep came slowly, and my thoughts drifted.

If we were successful, would our climb be considered just another gymnastic feat? Would failure, whether by a hairsbreadth or a calamity, make us look foolish to have even attempted the climb? We asked no rescue, and none was expected. How different our situation might be if, as in Switzerland, a téléphérique went up Mount Dickey and a rescue crew was even now lowering a cable. How many men, how many planes, how many changes would it take to destroy our remote experience in this alpine sanctuary?

Mount Dickey, unlike the majority of the McKinley massif, was not in a national park. It was currently unprotected but was included in a large southern extension proposed for Mount McKinley National Park. On an earlier expedition I had seen no threat of development to the lands that constituted the southern extension, and I doubted the need for official protection. I suspected that the minimal development that always comes in a national park's wake might be more damaging to the region than leaving it alone.

I've since changed my mind; I had drawn a romantic comparison between this land and Yosemite National Park. I had seen the Ruth Gorge as Yosemite had been in the Pleistocene epoch. Its ice hasn't melted, most of its peaks are unnamed, and it is rarely visited. In sharp contrast are the stores, golf course, jail, and bank of Yosemite proper. A national park in this part of Alaska had seemed grossly premature, but it now seems obvious that development throughout post-pipeline Alaska is imminent. The time for parkland is now. (In December 1978 the proposed extension was made into Denali National Monument.)

The existing Mount McKinley National Park is not plagued by the excess development so common in parks of the lower forty-eight. Its harsh climate and remoteness protect it, but a large share of the credit must go to its early superintendents. Three of the first four were men who had climbed Mount McKinley. Unlike most modern park managers, who acquire their jobs by administrative musical chairs, they had a hard-won, intimate appreciation for the land. Today most important park decisions come from Washington, but Harry Karstens, McKinley's first superintendent, was in a unique position. Not only had he led the first ascent of Mount McKinley, but he had also shared in the very birth of the idea of making a national park when he wintered north of the mountain with naturalist Charles Sheldon a decade before the park was created.

If John Muir could see Yosemite today, he would certainly question the idea of national parks. McKinley National Park, however, is a monument to the national park

The parkland north of Mount McKinley is perhaps North America's finest wildlife viewing area;
twenty-four hours of summer daylight and open vistas above timberline make it possible
to see even the most secretive nocturnal creatures.

idea and the goals of Sheldon and Karstens as they sat around campfires in the mountain's great shadow. The only indoor accommodations are at the park boundary. Fewer than one hundred campsites—and no other accommodations—exist along the 87-mile dirt road that crosses the park. Except for those with campsite registrations, all visitors must ride tour buses or walk through the park; private vehicles are banned. In contrast to the lifeless ice and rock of the Ruth Gorge, the park road traverses green, rolling tundra and spruce forests. Control of mechanized transportation keeps North America's finest wildlife viewing area much the way Sheldon saw it in 1906. During a single day in the park I saw moose, caribou, eagle, gyrfalcon, ptarmigan, porcupine, beaver, grizzly, Dall sheep, wolf, and, most remarkable of all, a lynx stalking a snowshoe hare forty feet away from me. To have this—and the Great Gorge—in a single national park would give McKinley the finest cross section of wilderness in any park in the world.

Grizzly mother and cub
(*Ursus arctos*), Sable Pass,
Mount McKinley National Park.

Caribou bulls (*Rangifer arcticus*) in Mount McKinley National Park.

Canada lynx (*Lynx canadensis*) stalking a snowshoe hare; photographed by the edge of the Teklanika River north of Mount McKinley, just after the Mount Dickey climb.

The morning after our bivouac in the storm, I peered out at a white world from high on Mount Dickey. A blizzard filled the air with snow, and rime ice clung to the rock above. It looked like photographs I'd seen of the Eigerwand in storm. I was wet but warm in my Fiberfill bag, and I suggested that we try to wait out the storm where we were. Both Dave and Ed wanted to head for the summit. I was worried about technical climbing with icy ropes, but descending 4000 feet in a storm was out of the question, and we had no inkling of how long it would last. Conditions could get much worse before they got better. Because we were running low on food, we agreed to continue climbing.

Using our only crampons and ice axe, Dave took the lead, and we soon came to a sudden juncture with dark, stratified, metamorphic rock held in place by ice and snow. Above, the angle of the face averaged sixty degrees, and the surface was about half rock and half snow, although much of what looked like snow turned out to be ice. We regretted not having more ice axes and crampons but, on the other hand, they might have slowed us down on the two previous days of rock climbing.

How totally different from our beginning on dry rock and a sunny day! It was as though we had switched to a different mountain on a different continent. We climbed roped together in a claustrophobic world of blowing snow, with visibility often less than one hundred feet. Our rate of progress slowed to a vertical crawl. Even Ed dropped his ever-present smile to say, "I don't like this. It seems real dangerous."

Dave, on the other hand, exuded confidence as his clawed feet led the way over icy black rock. He smiled and made quick decisions, seemingly totally in control of the situation. He was carrying a detailed photo of the face, now crumpled like a handkerchief, and occasionally he stopped to correlate features. As we moved higher we found progressively less rock and more snow, and finally we came to a place where everything above was white. Dave announced that we were close to the top. Estimating the angle would ease off in fifty feet or so, he climbed directly up steep ice and soon became a dark shadow in the snowy tempest. After climbing one hundred fifty feet without seeing an end to the ice, he retreated.

Ice from Dave's footsteps crashed down on Ed and me, but did not hurt us because we wore hardhats. Our smiles had entirely vanished by now; we were cold and disillusioned in the blowing storm, perhaps even lost. We began traversing hundreds of feet to the south, searching for a weakness in the continuous ice wall. We wanted rock outcrops for belays and piton protection, but rock was the exception and snow the rule. Our diagonal traverse angled upward, and Dave occasionally stopped to belay us individually over steep sections. I slogged through deep snow and climbed over a small cornice onto unexpected level ground. Dave shook hands with me, saying he thought we were on top. But where? We were in a white-out.

Ed soon joined us. At first we didn't agree on which direction to head on the broad summit plateau, but we decided to walk blindly south. Suddenly, through the storm, a tall flagpole appeared with a large, red flag blowing in the wind. I stared at it in disbelief: Who could have put such a thing near the summit of Mount Dickey? It hadn't been there a week before. We must not be in the right place. It took only a few seconds for these thoughts to race through my mind, and as I took another step, my error of perspective became obvious. It was one of our four-foot-tall willow wands with a small red ribbon, glowing from the shadowless murk of a white-out.

As we continued across the plateau, new wands appeared like tail lights out of fog until we came to our tiny cache. Two ice axes for the descent; one two-man tent, crowded for three, but luxurious compared with our previous nights' accommodations; and two days worth of freeze-dried food. These meager things were a pot of gold, and we were soon resting in the tent, tired, cold, satisfied.

The summit ramparts of
Mount Dickey's southeast face.

# 11 / *The Cirque of the Unclimbables*

IN THE SUMMER OF 1972, my friend Jim McCarthy and I flew in his small plane toward Jim's favorite spot on earth—the Cirque of the Unclimbables, an isolated group of granite peaks in the Logan Mountains of Canada's Northwest Territories. Located in a completely roadless area larger than California, the cirque is so remote that at the time of our visit fewer than twenty-five people had ever set foot there, although it is more spectacularly beautiful than any place I have seen in the national parks of North America.

Jim and I had just returned from an unsuccessful attempt on the Moose's Tooth in Alaska, and he assured me that the Logan Mountains, although at the same latitude, had far better weather than the Alaska Range. He had first visited the area a few years earlier, making the first ascent of Lotus Flower Tower in several warm, twenty-hour days. After a wretched spell of Alaskan rain and snow, we were ready for such a sunny paradise.

Our flight in Jim's Cessna over the vast, unpopulated reaches of the North provided a classic contrast between timeless nature and timebound man. The little plane was fully equipped for instrument flying. Often we slipped into the translucent void of a cloud bank, and I would watch Jim scan the panel and recreate in his mind the dynamic perspective of his craft moving across the landscape. Gradually I began to realize the limits of the various devices. When a call to an airport gave us a new barometer reading, Jim dialed it into the altimeter. The needle moved up. The plane did not. It was theoretically possible to read 2000 feet of ground clearance on a gauge a split second before slamming into the side of a mountain. The magnetic compass wigged and wagged as we passed near ore bodies. Nothing was absolute, I thought to myself, except time. Every thirty-six seconds, a new digit snapped into the hundredth's place on the gauge that registered hours.

But how absolute is the human conception of time? As we flew north across Canada, the dwindling number of settlements below us made it seem as if we were returning to a time long past in the United States. Calgary, a potential Canadian Los Angeles, quickly sprawled into a checkerboard of farms. The fields were dotted with small patches of forest, the only remnants of what was once an unbroken expanse of woodlands and lakes. Gradually the farms grew fewer until they became islands in a sea of lakes and forest, and in the Yukon, signs of man became still less frequent. Regardless of the regular ratcheting of the hour gauge, we were traveling backward, not forward, in time.

We landed the plane on the dirt airstrip of a small mining town. On a hillside above a long valley was the open pit. Ten-ton Euclid trucks howled back and forth on the Z-shaped road from the pit to the groaning and clanking processing mill in town. Pipes gushed black water into siltation ponds. Abandoned cars, empty oil drums, bits of lumber, and sewage formed a wreath around the town; tungsten and people were the only things carried out. A portly woman in her forties came riding down the hill on a

A trap basin filled with glacial silt created this level meadow under Mount Harrison Smith in the Cirque of the Unclimbables.

Lotus Flower Tower and Parrot Beak Peak
rise above lush green meadows.

A textbook example of a U-shaped glacial valley
in the Logan Mountains.

motorcycle. We met her later in the mess hall and learned that she was the cook for the single men living in the dormitories. She offered us food and coffee, and I commented on both the quality and quantity. "The boys get lots of good food and high pay," she replied. "They have to. A person needs that and more up here or else he'll go crazy. In the winter it sometimes goes seventy below, and the days are only four hours long. Most everyone has snowmobiles. In the summer people play baseball, go hiking, swimming—I ride a motorcycle, you know. A person has to have something else besides working. Why one fellow, he worked lots of overtime and did nothing but work, eat, and sleep. We warned him, but he wouldn't listen. They carried him out of here in a straightjacket."

An hour later we were in a jet helicopter, crossing icefields and snowy ridges on our way to the heart of the mountain range. Blue lakes lay below peaks in glacier-carved bowls. Far below the hanging alpine valleys were the trenches of the main rivers. The long hours of summer sun had melted the surface of the permafrost, changing level valley floors into impassable brush-tangled bogs that formed moats around the granite cathedrals in the center of the range.

The helicopter deposited us and our pile of gear in an alpine meadow and flew off. We planned a multi-day ascent of nearby Parrot Beak Peak and brought food for five days; the helicopter was to return on the fifth. Granite towers thousands of feet high loomed over the small meadow where we pitched our tent.

That evening I took a long walk into the next valley. From the air the vegetation had appeared uniformly green, but on closer inspection, the verdant grasses and mosses proved to be merely the dominant color in a melange of hues. The north sides of the rocks were splotched with colorful lichens; the south sides carpeted with thick mats of yellow moss. Streams were gray, not blue, because they were laden with glacial silt. Wildflowers grew in profusion on the meadowed benches. Rivulets snaked through the meadows and dipped off into the distance. I felt like an intruder as my footsteps squashed down the living mat.

I walked through a meadow decorated with tremendous squared boulders. One gigantic rock was split in three parts and through a narrow crack I could watch clouds swirling around the tops of towers. It gave me the unmistakable impression of being in a natural Stonehenge. Timberline was at only 4000 feet, and this meadow was far above the last trees. I saw marmots, finches, ptarmigans, and plenty of signs of mountain goats. I was surprised to find a dwarfed spruce growing behind a boulder in less than two inches of caribou moss. Although it had more than twenty sets of limbs, it was no more than eight inches tall. I would have taken for granted the most stately spruce, but this lone, small tree caught my attention and made me wonder how long it could last.

Morning dawned gray and cloudy. Jim and I agreed to delay our multi-day ascent and instead chose to climb a shorter but fine-looking buttress on the highest peak in the region, Mount Sir James McBrien. After three hours of unroped scrambling, we reached the beginning of technical climbing. A few hundred feet higher we came to a steep headwall. It was my turn to lead. Climbing here required a more cautious attitude than in a more accessible region; in case of injury or sickness, one might wait a long time to be evacuated. My feet began to twitch involuntarily, and I placed three pitons within arm's reach to protect one move over a difficult 5.10 ceiling.

Reaching the summit early in the evening, we saw a storm advancing from the other side of the peak. The complex descent on the easiest side of the peak involved traversing narrow ledges and kicking steps down snow-filled couloirs. Lower down we found fresh goat tracks and followed them onto a well-worn trail across grassy ledges. As we rounded a corner, I spotted a family of five goats ascending a nearby ridge. It was ten o'clock that night before we reached our tent in the rain.

It was still raining the next morning, and it continued for three more days without stopping. Around noon on the third day, Jim discovered that our beautiful meadow was fast becoming a lake. Although we had chosen the highest piece of ground, it was only six inches above the overall level; the water was rising fast and we were already on an island. Within five minutes we were furiously digging trenches with ice axes, defending our little portable environment against an onslaught of silt-laden water— the same waters which had created the meadow from a trap basin in the glacial moraine. It didn't work; the water was coming from every direction, faster than we could drain it with our crude tools. We paused to take stock of the situation and then spotted the main source of the water—a large stream pouring down the hillside just above the meadow. We concentrated our efforts there, building dams and trenching until we had altered the course of the stream to avoid the meadow completely.

Mount Sir James McBrien. Our climb ascended the prow seen on the skyline.

A young mountain goat (*Oreamnos americanus*) learns to climb by the school of hard knocks. In this photo, junior does a slow and awkward job of climbing a chimney 1000 feet up Mount Harrison Smith as his mother observes from above.

Here, the mother goat has moved down and is butting junior off the ledge. He tumbled fifty feet and appeared to be headed for certain death on the rocks below when he stopped himself on a smooth slab, got up unhurt, and climbed back up to his family in much better style.

An adult mountain goat climbs a vertical crack with easy motions and rippling muscles. Human climbers tried this spot, found it to be difficult 5.9 climbing, and used ropes and pitons for safety.

It would be nice to be able to say that we considered all the alternatives and chose one that was both practical and environmentally sound. However, I can't recall either of us suggesting that we simply move up onto the rocks and huddle under a tarp. How ironic that we who talked of preserving this place were busy trenching and damming at the first threat of getting wet. We even felt proud of our efforts. I finally understood how Floyd Dominy must have felt when he dedicated Glen Canyon Dam. All the same, I was horrified at my thoughts. Just a week earlier, flying over endless miles of woodland, I had experienced similar feelings when I found myself thinking, "Why are they cutting all that beautiful timber in California when they could be logging up here and nobody would miss it?" I quenched the thought immediately but recognized that for a moment I had experienced the frontier ethic of the North.

There was nothing to do now but wait in the tent. I teased Jim about his weather prophecy. He said the rain would quit soon, but I noticed him toying with his dismantled survival rifle and began to consider the serious possibility that we might be trapped here long enough to need it. When we awoke the next morning it was snowing. The clouds parted for a brief glimpse of the cliffs, and the scene was wild beyond description. Towers plastered in white loomed somberly out of the mist. A foot of snow lay on our meadow, and the goat paths on the mossy ledges were buried. Falling snowflakes dampened the acoustics of the cirque; except for the roar of an occasional avalanche, all was still.

The sixth day passed. Our food supply was very low, and we talked about what we could do if the helicopter never came. It might take us weeks to hike the fifty miles of brush and marshes between our cirque and the mine town. Suddenly I was no longer in a comfortable living room thumbing through a picture book of wilderness images. Here, in trouble, the value of civilization came clear. The embarrassing pride we felt over damming the stream, my flash of faulty logic about logging the North, and our present helplessness all began to fit together. I needed the tools of civilization. What did I have that I could do without? My mountain boots? My food? My sleeping bag? Without the umbilical cord to civilization that these things represented, I would be in bad shape. Back home, I had been lulled into false confidence in my own survival abilities by the nearness of civilization. I could reach habitation in two days of hiking from the most remote area in California.

In strict terms, much of what passes for a "wilderness experience" is counterfeit. Once in a while someone really does make a break for a short time—often it is accidental, termed "exposure," and results in a visit to a hospital. The "ruggedness" of a wilderness experience is not merely the physical effort involved, but the chance that the conditions of nature will exceed the capabilities of the equipment we bring with us. In other words, we risk being thrown into a true wilderness situation, one that modern people carefully avoid by special equipment, clothing, and rations.

Jim and I had brought an element of the technological world into the backcountry. Mountain tents do considerably less damage than many other kinds of portable environments, such as recreational vehicles, but even the most adaptable self-contained travelers, wilderness backpackers, leave their marks. Footsteps gradually wear footpaths; campfires gradually develop into permanent campsites, and the pursuit of the unknown sooner or later becomes a section in a guidebook. Even though backpackers are equipped to deal with a far wider set of circumstances than are

Tombstone Meadow, Cirque of the Unclimbables.

recreational vehicles, when the limits of their adaptability are exceeded they must either suffer or change the land to suit their needs, as we had chosen to do by trenching and damming.

In the natural world, an animal must adapt to its environment or perish. Civilization implies adapting the environment to human needs; much of the appeal of wilderness is that it can return people to the primeval situation to which humans are adapted. Keeping equipment down to a few simple items is one step toward this goal, but many people become more concerned with the means than the ends. Equipment is counted and compared like batting averages. The differences between various brands of equipment are far down the list of things that the modern, urban person needs to know in order to understand and enjoy the wilderness.

I peered outside the tent into a mist-shrouded dreamland of meadows, streams, and granite towers. A heavy rain was washing the snow from the meadow, but it was still snowing on the summits. The scene was magnificent, but I longed to be back in the mining town, though a week earlier I had scoffed at its prefabs, snowmobiles, and life styles. Once again the ethic of the North had caught up with me; it is hard to consider the intrinsic value of wilderness while it is a real adversary. In the United States, we are beginning to realize that our wildlands are finite, but in the Northwest Territories, an earlier spirit prevails. The people of the North are not wrong, any more than Americans were wrong to drive cars without smog devices in 1935, or to shoot buffalo when there were millions of them. Modern pioneers are living in a different age. Their daydreams are still of the future, and their frontier heroes have modern equipment. Today's Abraham Lincoln lives in a log cabin with central heating and a freezer full of moose. Today's Snowshoe Thompson has treads and makes rather more noise. And today's Davy Crockett—I met him in person, in Alaska—dynamites coyotes from his airplane. "Thirty-dollar bounty and you get to keep the pelt, you know."

My mental ramblings might not solve the problems of the developing North; but I did gain an increased awareness of how thoroughly we are trapped in our own time—I in mine, and the pioneers of this land in theirs. They must live through the same mistakes made by earlier pioneers before they can realize what they have lost. As for me, I still had to think in terms of basic survival. There was a helicopter buzzing in the back of my consciousness, and I hoped it would soon appear in reality.

The eighth morning dawned gray. Rain was intermittent, and fog hung low in the distant river valleys. Clouds still veiled the summits of the peaks. I put on my wet boots and stepped outside. Every watercourse was full. I grabbed my pack and a camera and announced that I was going for a walk. I'd gone only a hundred yards when the humming of the water was drowned out by a gradually increasing noise; I barely beat the helicopter to the tent. Suddenly time was of the highest value. Minutes ticked by at hundreds of dollars per hour as the helicopter waited for us to dismantle our camp. Darting around the meadow, we must have resembled the frantic, choppy characters in an early silent film. The pilot seemed puzzled that we took the time to bag up garbage and tie it into the baskets.

As we rose into the air, we had a view of the lower meadow completely submerged in water. We were witnessing the forces of its creation still at work today. But the silt-laden water was prevented by our earthworks from reaching the meadow where we had camped. We had been thoroughly conditoned to pick up garbage, even at great cost; but we had not thought of tearing down the dams during our expensive rush to return to civilization. Unconsciously, we had placed a dollar value on nature's chosen course for a mountain stream. I looked back at the sheer 2000-foot face of Proboscis, as impressive as Yosemite's Half Dome, following the clean granite with my eyes until it abruptly merged with jumbled red rock. A contact-metamorphic zone: what every prospector seeks when hunting copper, lead, and gold. The list could continue— tungsten, molybdenum, silver, zinc—but the meaning was the same. Call it progress, manifest destiny, the ethic of the North—time could all too easily catch up to these mountains.

When I returned home I wrote about our visit without using a single place name. I wanted to emphasize the nature of the experience rather than the place itself, and I feared that the area might be damaged by overuse if my article attracted too many visitors. Through word of mouth and mountaineering journals, the Cirque has since become well known to climbers all over the world, and the experience is no longer the same. There is garbage in the meadows and the solitude is gone. What I choose to remember is the feeling of moving backward through time, back to the kind of experience enjoyed by the early explorers of the Grand Canyon, of Yellowstone, the Grand Tetons, or Yosemite; back to the time before these scenic wonders became islands of wild country surrounded by cities, roads, and farms. Finding this experience in North America in the 1970s was the journey's greatest reward.

Stream in Tombstone Meadow.

# 12 / *Around Mount McKinley on Skis*

I N 1906 the explorer Frederick Cook reported that his fast, light expedition had made the first ascent of Mount McKinley in only eight days. Cook's climb was soon discredited, however, and the rest of his life unfolded as if the hoax had been branded on his forehead. His claim to have reached the North Pole in 1909 was disbelieved mainly on the basis of the Mount McKinley episode, while Admiral Peary's polar jaunt, reported to the world at the same time and with even less documentation, was accepted as authentic. (The consensus of present-day authorities is that neither explorer actually reached the Pole, although both spent considerable time very far north.) McKinley figured yet again in Cook's life, when the climbing hoax was mentioned in a judge's verdict convicting him of selling useless land in Wyoming as oil property during the Teapot Dome scandal. Cook spent more than a decade in federal prison; his confiscated lands, in which his life savings had been invested, eventually produced more oil than he had ever promised prospective buyers. On his deathbed, he was pardoned by FDR.

Like other explorers, Cook named many of his geographical discoveries, but his names for the most part have disappeared from modern maps, and his actual achievements are all but forgotten. One of his more unusual adventures was a land circumnavigation of Mount McKinley in 1903. Up to that time, the approaches to the highest point in North America were unknown, and Cook spent four months making a 540-mile orbit along rivers, through forests, across passes and glaciers. For three-quarters of a century to come, no one else circled the mountain on the ground.

When I circled McKinley in a small plane in 1972, I was amazed by the interconnecting pattern of five major glaciers, each one longer than any in the Nepal Himalaya. They flow down the peak's flanks and abruptly turn to form a ring of ice ninety miles in circumference and shaped like the outline of a cottonwood leaf. McKinley's great circle of moving ice, entirely above timberline, is unique among the 20,000-foot peaks of the world. The great circle would have become a popular ski-mountaineering route years ago, were it not for one problem: the mountain's three major buttresses trisect the route at elevations of 10,000 to 12,000 feet. This makes the difficulties involved in circling the mountain even greater than those of climbing it. In the last two decades, several groups attempted the circle, but were forced to retreat by frostbite or technical difficulties. My own eagerness to ski such a great natural route was tempered by the realization that packs might weigh 100 pounds, a broken ski could be devastating, and certain icefalls might prove impassable.

In 1978 I was invited to join the Mount McKinley Great Circle Expedition. Ned Gillette, an Olympic cross-country skier in 1968, had full financing from some Norwegian ski companies to attempt an "orbit" far tighter than Cook's. It would be the first within the limits of the peak's glacial systems and would follow the precise route I had studied from the air. Had the choice been mine, I would have brought sturdy downhill skis with mountaineering bindings, but Ned wanted to prove the

Descending an icefall on skis into the Don Sheldon Amphitheater, just outside the border of Mount McKinley National Park.

strength of the light touring skis and narrow, fifty-millimeter racing binding that he used on packed tracks. He had already used "skinny skis" to cross Ellesmere Island, the land mass nearest the North Pole. Our foursome consisted of Ned and myself plus Alan Bard and Doug Weins, who had skied Ellesmere in 1977. All of us had the climbing experience necessary to cross the three icy ridges that separate the glaciers.

We estimated that the Great Circle would take about three weeks and require two food caches. On April 7 bush pilot Cliff Hudson landed us on the Kahiltna Glacier, just outside the boundary of Mount McKinley National Park. Each of us was in shape for cross-country skiing and for carrying big loads—our packs weighed ninety pounds— but not for both together. We skied off with all the grace of newborn calves, and instead of linked figure eights, our tracks down the first easy slope resembled a child's by-the-numbers sketch, each circled number corresponding to a crater in the snow.

Three days and one storm later, we reached our first obstacle, Kahiltna Pass on the West Buttress. It was −12° F as we started up what appeared to be a forty-degree snowslope; we quickly discovered that a thin frost layer lightly covered blue ice un-

Skiers above a route
that wouldn't go:
a fork of the Ruth Glacier
below Traleika Col.

Peaks of the Great Gorge
of the Ruth Glacier
as seen from 11,000 feet
on Traleika Ridge.

derneath. I led a full rope length on front points without finding a belay. With our second and last rope tied on, I reached a snow-covered crevasse about two feet wide. I couldn't place a secure screw in the rotten ice, and my axe sank too easily into the powdery snow outside the crevasse. I dug my way inside and sat on a snowbridge directly over the rope; if the screw and axe pulled out, I planned to become a human anchor by jumping in.

When we reached the crest of the Alaska Range, we could see beyond peaks coated in a winter armor of blue ice toward endless white plains to the north. Below us, the Peters Glacier stretched into the distance like a smooth highway. To gain the head of the glacier, we descended several thousand feet of steep snow. The surface of the glacier was a veritable frozen ocean of icy waves and swells; a ground blizzard driven by high winds added a mystical haze to the landscape.

We found little time to contemplate the great beauty of the scene, however, for without metal ski edges, we fell down repeatedly. Alan took an especially bad header and dislocated his shoulder. He stood up in pain, popped the joint back in with his own tug, and held his arm helplessly against his chest. We set up camp immediately, wondering if two us would have to make at least a week's journey out to summon a rescue.

In the morning Alan was able to continue, but on foot instead of on skis. Luckily we were now on a section of hard windslab rather than the powder snow of earlier days. That afternoon Alan decided to try skiing, timidly on gentle slopes. He was afraid of losing control on the downhill runs, but the conditions made this impossible. The surface of the entire lower glacier was underlain with depth hoar—bottomless sugar snow formed in cold, dry conditions—and for the next two days we were held to a pace of two miles in ten hours. Typically, we alternated from knee-deep snow to sudden holes of thigh-deep crystals that rolled underfoot like ball bearings. This resulted in frequent falls, always onto one's back, followed by the tiring struggle to get up again. I was reminded of a cartoon that showed a backpacker lying on his back by a trail, his arms and legs flailing, and one observer commenting to another: "I hear they die if you don't turn them over."

From the wretched Peters Glacier, we headed up Gunsight Pass and onto the Muldrow Glacier. The depth hoar was gone, and we had easy sailing for several days as we turned up the Traleika Glacier toward the East Buttress of McKinley. We were through the easy half of our circle, and by this time our individual roles in the expedition had become clear. Ned was our leader. His job was to make decisions when there was a difference of opinion on how to proceed, but we always wanted to do the same things; so instead he busied himself with watching his carefully planned dream unfold. I was our logistics officer, responsible for such key decisions as which way to aim the tent door each night. Each morning, with the consistency of the rising sun, a brisk wind blew from the exact direction the door was aimed. Alan Bard was to have been our humorist, but since everyone joked, he contributed his laughter to the general supply. Doug Weins, the lightest member of the party, quickly earned the title of chief crevasse locator. Regardless of whether he was first or last on the rope at any given time, he faithfully punched his body through the snow to discover dangerous holes for us. As it happened, he had the greatest fear of crevasses.

The East Buttress was the next major problem to overcome, and we spent six hours ascending it over 2500 feet of steep ice and snow. The descent route down the Ruth Glacier side was even more continuously steep, so we decided to bivouac on top rather than risk getting caught on the headwall, which averaged seventy degrees for a thousand feet. We pitched our tent on the narrow ridge crest as clouds swirled around us blocking our view. Just before sunset they lifted to reveal one of the most beautiful landscapes on earth. From an elevation of nearly 11,000 feet we looked directly across the glacier at the granite and ice of the Moose's Tooth, Mount Dickey, and Mount Huntington. The moon rose into a clear sky that turned pink, then lilac, and finally the indigo blue of an Alaskan spring night.

The next morning we made the first committing rappel down the headwall. It was underlain with water ice, and placing anchors was a major problem. After we left our only two ice screws behind as rappel anchors, we relied entirely on fixing the rope around bollards shoveled out of the snow cover or chopped laboriously into the ice. When the afternoon sun hit the slope, we became concerned about avalanche danger. As we neared the base and the angle lessened, Ned unroped and rushed out of reach of potential slides. Alan and I followed. Walking in our tracks, Doug dropped into a bergschrund and disappeared from sight except for the tips of his skis. It was just blind luck that the bergschrund was nearly full of snow, and Doug was able to climb out

A ground blizzard rips
across the frozen ocean of
the Peters Glacier on the
northwest side of
Mount McKinley.

without our help. When all four of us finally stood clear of the headwall, we jumped up and down in joyful relief. On returning from the expedition, we learned that we had been the first to cross the East Buttress. A British party in 1962 had crested the ridge, only to retreat after looking down the other side.

The next day began in trepidation and ended with joyful surprises. At first we felt closed in by the peaks and icefalls that separated our arm of the Ruth Glacier from the main trunk, but after some anxious searching a skiable route opened in front of us. Nearing the great Don Sheldon Amphitheater we crossed outside the national park boundary, into the unprotected public lands then under consideration as a southern extension of the park.

Around midday as we lunched on the open glacier, two loud noises interrupted our solitude. The first was a great avalanche, falling 4000 feet and rolling half a mile across the flats before it stopped uncomfortably close to us. The second was even louder and nearer: An airplane buzzed us at fifteen feet. Now that we had entered an area where low flights and air drops were permitted, Cliff Hudson was checking our progress before leaving our final cache next to Don Sheldon's Mountain House. As the plane passed overhead, we were bombarded by falling objects marked with yellow streamers. The others rushed for cans of beer, and I found a letter from my lady in California. When I opened it, a wildflower fell out into my hand.

In the midst of this sterile landscape, the tiny flower affected me powerfully. Like animals on the hunt, mountaineers must rely almost entirely on immediate sensations. The wildflower in my hand freed my thoughts from the present and set them on a track of wild speculation; I began to see both the surrounding scene and my companions through the veil of time. I wondered if the same flower had once grown during an ancient interglacial period in the place where I now stood. Here in the Ruth Gorge was a glimpse of how the Sierra and the Rockies must have looked during the height of the Pleistocene glaciations; and the same sort of cooperative behavior that primitive man had developed for hunting and defense was evident in our group. Modern equipment couldn't hide what we left behind us each morning; a depression in the snow surrounded by tracks and droppings, not unlike the bedding area of any large mammal. Traveling this glacial world forced us to recognize our primeval heritage. I recalled John Muir's feeling of "an unexplainable mysticism" while in the presence of glaciers, and the more explicit theory of the modern biologist Valerius Geist, who discounts Africa as the major source of recent human evolution and believes that the coming of the ice in more northerly latitudes was the major factor that forced our ancestors to cooperate in groups and develop their brains.

Holding a flower on an ocean of ice, I wondered if the joy I felt in the cold, inhospitable world might be rooted in my genes. Perhaps our venture, away from our homes and loved ones over primeval valleys of ice, somehow replicated an archetypal way of human life. A sense of unfathomable nearness pulsed through me and the world closed in. Then I looked toward the Gateway to the Great Gorge. Vague images from times I never knew became intertwined with explicit memories of earlier visits to the gorge, and then the moment was gone.

Continuing on across the Ruth Glacier, we reached the Mountain House, where we spent a blissful night in the comfort of the cabin, followed by a rest day. Our second and final cache lay buried near the house in two cartons. I tore rapaciously into the first box, but Alan suggested waiting before we opened the second. On Alan's suggestion, Ned and I went off together on an afternoon ski tour to the mouth of the Gorge. We returned to a cabin brightly decorated for a surprise party. Alan and Doug had packed the second box in Ned's Vermont basement and had included all the trimmings for Ned's thirty-third birthday. Balloons, crepe streamers, and party favors hung from the ceiling. To the strains of "Happy Birthday," Ned was presented with an endless array of things-you-always-wanted-on-a-glacier: party hats, whistles, a toy telephone, a plastic gun that spun tops into the air, popcorn, a cake with candles, and a tall bottle of whiskey. Just then a group of younger climbers on their first remote expedition happened on the scene; they couldn't have looked more surprised had they been invited into a spaceship. The party continued well into the night.

A moonlit night at Don Sheldon's "Mountain House" on the Ruth Glacier under Mount McKinley. The only building in thousands of square miles of alpine wildlands, it was constructed entirely of materials flown in by ski plane.

A day of waiting out a storm, plus two easy days up the west fork of the Ruth Glacier, brought us to a cul-de-sac underneath Ruth Gap, the lowest point between the Ruth and Kahiltna Glaciers. Festooned with overhanging ice, this low point had wisely not been called a pass. To the best of our knowledge it had never been crossed, and it still hasn't. We opted for a longer, less steep route that crested the South Buttress of McKinley at 12,000 feet. Luckily we had acquired two more ice screws from a Mount Huntington expedition; these aided our passage up a section of 60-degree blue ice. That day ended in the middle of a broken icefall on the Kahiltna side of the buttress. Two long overhanging rappels were necessary to connect a route through the giant seracs. One ended hanging over space, and I had to swing back and forth in order to sink an axe in the far wall of a deep crevasse.

On our nineteenth day we found an easy path through the steep lower icefall onto the east fork of the Kahiltna Glacier. When we joined the main glacier we spotted some ski tracks that were nearly imperceptible until the light hit the snow at just the right angle. It took us a while to realize that these tracks were our own. We had closed the "Great Circle."

Our expedition lacked the great geographical climax of a summit; like polar explorers, we stood in a snowy expanse where one spot looked like the next. Our goal was to come back to a starting point, not to reach the heights and turn around. By itself, the patch of snow where we stood was insignificant; what counted was how we had come to reach it. As Ned simply put it: "We have reached completion."

# 13 / A One-Day Ascent of Mount McKinley

W HEN we became partners for two unique Alaskan adventures, Ned Gillette and I hardly knew each other. Chance had brought us together in Vermont when Ned had driven forty miles on a winter night to attend my lecture on high-altitude climbing. As we talked after the lecture, we both felt an unusually strong bond of understanding and trust. Ned invited me to join his ski expedition to circle Mount McKinley (described in the preceding chapter); I in turn asked him to join me immediately afterwards in an attempt to climb McKinley in a single day from its western base at 10,000 feet. Although we had no way of foreseeing it then, our mutual trust soon was to undergo an extreme test.

After the ski orbit went like clockwork, Ned and I camped at the base of McKinley's west buttress, waiting for a clear day. When it came we were off at 2:30 A.M. in the April twilight of the Alaska Range. By 5 A.M. we had reached Windy Corner at 13,400 feet where the temperature was −20° F. Instead of the soft snow I had found on a previous climb, we encountered windblown snow and patches of blue ice. Just as we stopped to switch from skis to crampons, Ned's ski edges suddenly slid, and he plummeted toward a cliff, sixty feet away. Ned and I were roped together with our ice axes cleverly lashed to our packs, well out of reach. In the seconds before the rope pulled tight, I jammed the tip of a ski pole into the ice in a futile attempt at a self-arrest; then a tremendous jerk at my waist launched me toward Ned's falling form. I saw myself headed for a last, long ride in space—a vision as ghastly as Slim Pickens riding down on the bomb in the final scene of "Dr. Strangelove."

A mere arm's length from the cliff, I stopped—face first against Ned's steel ski edges. Our individual actions, unknown to each other, had cooperated to save our lives. My self-arrest had failed, but not before it slowed Ned for a split second, enabling him to grab a fixed rope left by an earlier expedition as he fell head first on his back. Adrenalin gave his gloved hand a death grip on the quarter-inch polypropylene. Had he not stopped with his skis in the air, I would have fallen past him and pulled us both off the cliff.

My hand went to my face, and my fingers felt a gaping hole where I had once had a mouth. My front teeth were missing, and my lower lip was split, spread to my chin like blinders on a horse's face. With the gentle confidence that had gained my trust in Vermont, Ned said, "Don't move until we figure this out; I'm holding us with a rope in my hand behind my back."

Late that same day a plastic surgeon in Anchorage put my face back together. We had managed our own rescue by climbing and skiing twelve miles down the peak and its glaciers to a landing area for bush pilots. Once, Ned slipped into a crevasse behind me, and I pulled so hard that he popped up like toast out of a toaster.

While my injuries healed, Ned and I spent hours on the telephone between Vermont and California discussing whether we could have made the climb if the fall

Sunset from 14,000 feet
on Mount McKinley.

Avalanche chute
above the Kahiltna Glacier.

had not occurred. We didn't wait long to find out; a month after the accident, we returned to Mount McKinley for another try.

Normal expeditions take a month to climb the peak. What made us think we could do it so quickly? Although we were more fit than most men in their mid-thirties, we were no more so than the thousands of men, women, and children who can run twenty-six mile marathons in less than three hours. Although I run five to twelve miles of hills every day, my efforts to move my fireplug-shaped body twenty-six miles at a time never bettered three-and-a-half hours. To climb McKinley in one day, I estimated that we would need to expend the effort of four marathons back to back—sixteen to twenty hours on the move. The comparison with running cannot be taken further. The runner has the security of knowing he can quit by simply walking off the course; the climber must find security elsewhere. Big expeditions rely on portable environments, survival equipment, and manpower. For two men with day packs on the coldest 20,000-foot peak on earth, security must come from within, from self-knowledge.

Learning to combine extreme mental and physical stresses is a major reward of climbing mountains. Ned and I felt that we had the necessary blend of stamina, altitude experience, climbing skills, will power, and knowledge of the surroundings to try McKinley with no more equipment than could fit into a day pack.

Conventional expeditions move at a snail's pace because, like that animal, they carry their homes on their backs. Encumbered with hundreds of pounds per person of food, fuel, and arctic survival gear, these groups follow the tradition established by the 1913 first ascent of Mount McKinley.

The story of the first ascent is relatively uneventful, with the exception of an astonishing sight they saw from the top: a flagpole stood on the summit ridge of the 900-foot-lower north peak. Three years earlier, in 1910, an Alaskan Sourdough named Tom Lloyd mushed his dog team into Fairbanks, claiming that he had led his party of four from 10,000 feet to the summit of McKinley in a single day and had planted a fourteen-foot spruce flagpole on top. After an initial flurry of interest, the story was classed with legends of lost gold mines and Sasquatch sightings, but the verification of the pole by the 1913 party confirmed the tall tale as partial reality. It turned out that Lloyd had exaggerated his personal role. Weighing well over 200 pounds, he was not particularly fit and, in fact, had never ventured over 11,000 feet. His three companions, however, had indeed gone for the summit from a camp at 10,800 feet. Charley McGonagall, reputed to be the strongest man in the North, tired of carrying the pole and quit at 18,000 feet. Billy Taylor and Pete Anderson then took

Bald eagle (*Haliaetus leucocephalus*) in flight, near Mount McKinley.

the pole and reached the top of the north peak—an amazing 8500-foot climb in one day. They had spent three previous weeks shoveling and stomping a path to 16,000 feet before finally going for the top, and in this way they had inadvertently acclimatized themselves to levels well above their high camp. Their claim that they would have reached the true summit, had they known it to be higher, is entirely plausible.

If Taylor and Anderson had been credited with the true first ascent, subsequent McKinley climbs—and perhaps the entire history of American expeditionary climbing abroad—might have been based on their bold style. As it was, the Sourdough's saga became a Paul Bunyan tale repeated around campfires but not in real life. For sixty-eight years, no one attempted another one-day climb from a comparable altitude. Meanwhile, more than a thousand people had reached McKinley's summit using traditional heavy expeditions and high camps.

The Sourdough climb was the unwitting forerunner of the most modern style of high-altitude climbing, a sport that had moved up a blind alley for most of this century. Giant military-style expeditions hastened their own obsolescence by proving that any mountain on earth could be climbed—given enough time, equipment, money, and porter carries. The new challenge is to do great peaks in "alpine style," without fixed ropes, camps, high porters, or oxygen apparatus. An unsupported climber simply can't carry enough food and fuel to sustain himself for more than a few days on a big mountain; true alpine-style ascents must be done very fast, or not at all.

Four of the dozen highest peaks in the world have now been climbed in three days or less by fast, light expeditions. Although Mount McKinley is far lower in measured elevation than any of those, it is actually greater in vertical relief from timberline to summit. And its weather—the biggest unknown factor in any alpine-style ascent—is notoriously bad.

For two days after we had come up from sea level, Ned and I sat in the clouds at 10,000 feet, waiting for one perfect day to make our final push. Like King Midas lusting for gold, we wanted twenty-four hours of clear, still air on a peak that has the worst year-round climate of any non-polar spot on earth.

At noon on the third day the clouds lifted; the upper mountain gleamed against blue sky. Our day had arrived with a Midas touch, for we had counted on at least five days of acclimatization at 10,000 feet before dashing up to 20,000 feet. The forecast was for forty hours of rare calm, followed by a storm; if we let it pass, we might not get another clear spell before our ten days supply of food and fuel ran out. On the other hand, climbing too soon could be dangerous. Our one-day time frame was far from arbitrary. The extra weight of food and fuel needed for two days would probably push the climb into a third day. Pulmonary and cerebral edema, two forms of the often fatal "climber's bends" brought on by fatigue and sudden altitude gain, almost never start until twenty-four hours after stress; and descent is a sure cure in all but the most advanced cases. To get out of the clutches of extreme altitude in a single day was sound preventive medicine. But could we move that fast without acclimatization?

We tried to postpone a decision and sleep a few hours but anxiety kept us wide awake. At 9 P.M. on June 9, we shouldered day packs, stepped into our skis, and struck off. We made fast time, and the sun was just setting as we reached our old 13,400-foot high point at 11 P.M. The icy traverse where we had fallen was now covered with firm snow, but without exchanging a word we cached our skis for the descent and strapped

*144*

Ned Gillette at 16,500 feet
during the one-day climb.

crampons onto our boots. (Ned had devised a boot combination for us utilizing oversized "Superlight" summer mountaineering boots with thin foam inners from downhill ski boots, giving us more warmth than normal double boots at a fraction of the weight.) The four-hour Alaskan night held no threat of darkness, and we continued on.

At six in the morning we took our first long rest at the standard high camp at 17,300 feet. Just below, Ned had vomited from the altitude and fatigue and was unsure about continuing, but I was eager to keep going. I started our tiny stove next to an igloo, waking two climbers who had been sleeping inside. One of them complained in a strong British accent. Hot drinks, cheese, and warmth of the sun's first rays gave Ned the strength to continue, and we left before the other climbers emerged from the igloo. We climbed for two more hours to Denali Pass at 18,200 feet, where we paused on the crest of the Alaska Range under a sky of unbroken indigo in absolutely still air.

It was a day even better than our wildest dreams, but Ned was still feeling poorly and quietly announced that he wanted to quit. My heart sank. "We'll never have another chance like this," I told him. "Only 2000 feet and we're there, and it's still early morning." He assented, and we moved on, marching like wound-down toy soldiers.

At 19,000 feet two small figures approached from below as we lay sprawled in the snow resting, all dignity abandoned. The two men stopped and eyed the obviously unfit and out-of-place climbers at their feet, and one of them remarked, "Anyone who needs a rope up here dosen't belong on this mountain!" The British accent identified him as one of the men whose sleep we had interrupted at 17,300 feet. When we introduced ourselves, their attitude became friendlier. The Britisher, Nigel Gifford, had been on expeditions to Everest and Nuptse and was planning to look me up as a climbing partner in California. His companion, John Purdue, was a Canadian. Nigel's comment about the rope made Ned and I realize that we could do without the extra weight, so we left both rope and packs lying in the snow when we again set off. All four of us started out together, but because of Nigel and John's rest and acclimatization, Ned and I quickly were left behind. I soon began to feel like a zombie, while Ned's nausea disappeared. Our roles were being reversed and Ned was now the stronger, but our cooperative efforts kept us going.

As we neared 20,000 feet, we watched Nigel and John reach the summit, turn around, and start back down. When they stopped only a hundred feet below the top and didn't move for a long time, we wondered if something was wrong. We reached them half an hour later and found them sitting on a platform they had stamped into the steep slope, with their stove humming reassuringly in the still air. With the air of a proper British gentleman, Nigel inquired, "Would you like a cup of tea?"

We sipped and chatted for half an hour before continuing on a few minutes to the top. We were rewarded with a splendid view of the entire "Great Circle" of glaciers we had recently skied for the first time. Our climb had taken nineteen hours all told—nine for the 7300 feet to 17,300 and another nine, after a forty-five-minute rest, to make the last 3000 feet. The vertical distance we had covered was very nearly that from Mount Everest's base camp to its summit. The effort had required most of our strength, and as we started down, we moved like people with nerve injuries learning to walk—minds focused, but bodies responding with only a glimmer of their normal ability.

146

Sunset on Pioneer Ridge, Mount McKinley.

Ned occasionally had to help me over even slight rises in the terrain, and we inevitably fell asleep during brief rests, even on steep slopes. Whoever remained conscious longer would jerk the other awake with the rope.

Just before we reached the 17,300-foot camp, I checked my breathing, as I had at least once an hour since we had been above 17,000 feet. Slight gurgles in my chest indicated the beginnings of pulmonary edema; the symptoms had appeared twenty-three hours after my first exposure to increased altitude and stress—almost precisely as predicted by the experts.

The National Park Service has spent tens of thousands of taxpayers' dollars helicoptering edema victims off McKinley's upper slopes, and they advise climbers not to go too high too quickly. Statistics do show that slower parties run less risk of edema but fail to take into account the simple logic that fast, mobile parties have a far greater

Ned Gillette links turns through untracked powder on the Kahiltna Glacier—a difficult feat on Nordic skis with 50mm bindings.

Kahiltna Glacier and the Mount McKinley massif.

chance to reverse the course of the illness by prompt descent. Most rescues come after a climber has stayed in a high camp for a period of days—usually in bad weather, further delaying air rescue. We had no radio to summon a rescue and felt absolutely no need to call out, as we planned to descend quickly. When we reached high camp, we found Gifford and Purdue camped there with a large guided expedition. We were equipped to bivouac, but we gladly accepted their offer to join them for the night. Because the expedition had a radio, we decided not to mention the mild edema symptoms for fear of initiating an unnecessary rescue.

In the morning we climbed down to Windy Corner, where our skis were cached, and finished the descent with a splendid 3500-foot downhill run through icefalls and snow bowls. By the time we crawled into our tent at Kahiltna Pass, my edema had subsided. Ned and I sat watching storm clouds creep up the forty-six-mile length of the Kahiltna Glacier toward the mountain, and talked about our experience. It was our first real opportunity to relax and reflect; the pace of the climb had been too intense, and we had been far too busy monitoring the weather, our progress, and our bodies.

We agreed that we owed our success on this venture—and our lives on the first attempt—to our cooperative actions, our mutual trust, and our common will. This knowledge was its own reward, and we found satisfaction in having met the mountain on its own terms—penetrating its defenses with a few classic tools. It had not been our goal to start a speed competition on the mountain; we knew that our time would be bettered some day by people who had acclimatized longer and trained harder. We hoped that others would adopt the heritage of the sourdoughs, seeking simple ways of dealing with nature, rather than striving to overcome a mountain by a long siege. It was for this kind of experience that Ned and I had formed our partnership. Before we went to sleep, we talked of doing other fast and light expeditions in the ultimate range, the Himalaya.

# Epilogue

"I welcome wholeheartedly the advance of modern techniques
because it has widened the bounds of mountain adventure.
There was a time, long ago, when I was oppressed
by the thought that soon there would be no peaks to climb
and no new routes to explore.
But the more I travelled in the remoter ranges . . . the more
I realized how vast is the field of fresh endeavor. . . .
With the application of these new climbing and
survival techniques, the horizon is truly boundless."

ERIC SHIPTON
*That Untravelled World*

Storm over the Palisades, High Sierra.

Bouldering, in which the climber uses no technical equipment
but only boots and fingertips.

Two skiers and an avalanche
on Alaska's Kahiltna Glacier.

Split rock and cirrus cloud, Owens Valley, California.

A stormy sunrise on the crest of the Sierra Nevada.

# A NOTE ON THE PHOTOGRAPHY

To RECORD the spontaneity of high and wild experiences, I used only 35mm equipment. Taking large-format cameras into the wilderness is too much of a compromise with adventure for me. While I admire the clarity of images made with such cameras, their usefulness in photographing wilderness adventures is limited by their cumbersomeness, which makes it nearly impossible to capture a companion in the act of skiing or climbing. Without incredibly heavy lenses, they cannot photograph distant wildlife or scenes. For still scenes, I handle the 35mm camera as if it were a 4 × 5. Instead of taking a quick, handheld shot, I use a tripod and slow, fine-grained film; and I spend lots of time composing and selecting the right aperture for my desired zone of focus. Yet the same equipment gives me the freedom to record action as it occurs.

My basic equipment for going light is a Nikon FM with a 24mm and 105mm lens. Depending on the need, I also bring along one or more of the following lenses: 20mm, 35mm, 45mm, 55mm, 200mm, 400mm, 500mm, 600mm, as well as macro and perspective-control lenses. On photo assignments, or on any trip where photography is especially important, I carry two camera bodies. I keep one loaded with Kodachrome 25, the best transparency film for sharpness and latitude (the amount of detail a film can pick up in shadows and highlights). Its colors are less harsh than its cousin, Kodachrome 64, which I use in the second camera when extra film speed is needed for action, wildlife, or night photography.

I seldom use faster films, because unless the light is very even, films over ASA 100 tend to produce harsh-looking slides that end up in my wastebasket. I do not use "fish-eyes" or extreme telephotos because I wish to record what I see, not an image obviously altered by equipment.

The colors in this book are as real as photography and printing can make them. No filters were used to alter the tone of an entire scene, other than a very mild Nikon A2 that removes the bluish tint from shadows. A polarizer was used for about ten percent of these photographs. The aim in reproduction is to achieve the greatest possible fidelity to the originals, but because the inks used in printing do not produce exactly the same tones as the dyes that record color in film, some small differences are inevitable.

When taking photographs, I am always aware of how each natural color will appear on film. Only by consciously thinking about the limitations of the film can I visualize how the image will appear. Tones of red, for instance, vary greatly in different exposures of the same scene. True blacks are rarely seen by the eye; nearly every black silhouette in this book was actually illuminated with enough light to read by. Many beautiful sights are impossible to transfer onto film; rather than intrude my camera into an experience for no purpose, I simply enjoy them.

Wilderness photographs are like gems: the real and the synthetic are often indistinguishable. The photos in this book have, for me, a stamp of reality that I find missing in images I sometimes "create" on editorial or advertising assignments. Nearly all of my favorite photographs are ones that I was not seeking in the first place. The unexpected in nature always provides the greatest artistic opportunity, and capturing such a moment is rarely just the result of being in the right place at the right time. It is a blend of intuitive thinking and technical discipline, a coming together of the two halves of the brain to simultaneously see with an artist's eye while operating equipment precisely.

HIGH AND WILD

*was designed by Klaus Gemming, New Haven, Connecticut,*
*and printed in four-color process by*
*Princeton Polychrome Press, Princeton, New Jersey,*
*on Northwest's 80-lb. Vintage Gloss paper.*
*The text was set in Linofilm Sabon by*
*Finn Typographic Service, Stamford, Connecticut.*
*The book was bound by A. Horowitz & Son, Fairfield, New Jersey.*

SIERRA CLUB BOOKS